CHANGING THE STARS
A MEMOIR

Cody Renegar

Cody Renegar Books
LOS ANGELES, CALIFORNIA

Cody Renegar / Cody Renegar Books
www.codyrenegar.com

Cover Painting by Cody Renegar
Author Photographs by Craig MacLeod
Cover Design by Gus Yoo
Copy Editing and Book Production Stephanie Gunning
Book Layout © 2021 Book Design Templates

Special discounts are available on quantity purchases by corporations, associations, and others. For details, contact the publisher at the website above.

Changing the Stars / Cody Renegar. —1st ed.
ISBN 978-1-7365359-0-5 (paperback)
ISBN 978-1-7365359-1-2 (kindle ebook)

I am dedicating this book to my sister Sue, who has been my comforting constant in this totally inconsistent world. Her strength and love and unfaltering support have been more than enough fuel to send me to the stars!

CONTENTS

MESSAGE TO THE READER

All the information in this book is true. Some names and identifying details have been changed to protect certain individuals that were involved in these events.

ACKNOWLEDGMENTS

First and foremost, I am grateful to my sister Sue.

Of course, I also have to mention her daughter, Samantha. Seeing myself in the reflection of her eyes has always driven me to be the best me I could possibly be and to keep reaching for the stars! She has been the president of my fan club since the moment she was born and there was no way I was going to let her down.

If it were not for my son, Levi, and knowing that he was watching me more closely than anyone else, I don't believe I would have become the man I am today. Setting an example for him in absolutely every way has been a number one priority in my thoughts since the moment I knew he was coming into this world. Watching my son grow into the kind, loving, hardworking, caring, loyal, respectful man he is today has been my greatest pride. He chose a lovely partner, and they gave me three absolutely wonderful grandchildren. They are amazing parents and watching them all together gives me great comfort. I guess I did something right somewhere along the way.

My best friend, Jameson, has been my foundation for the past seventeen years. He has watched me struggle and climb and falter and fall yet he stood by my side with a kind and helping hand at every turn. My best friend has shown me unconditional and selfless love as he pushed me upwards and onward, all the while keeping my feet firmly on the ground.

I am also grateful for my phenomenal husband, Terry. This man has shown me what true love feels like. Since the moment I met him, I have wanted to be a better version of myself, every single day. He has shown me that true love will bring out the best in yourself if you allow it. He's selflessly puts me first in all that he does. He does not make a move without considering me first. I always feel like my husband is some sort of reward from the universe for persevering through the struggles of the first half of my life. Terry has taken my hand and literally shown me the world. We travel this entire planet together and try to share a little love along the way. I will forever be grateful to this man. In this life and the next.

The writing of this book was a process that took seven years because the material was difficult to revisit, akin to digging into a scar that needs to be reopened to heal properly. Among those who supported me I would like to highlight two.

Thank you to Amber King, who gave me the first feedback on the manuscript and told me she was crying when she read it. Hearing her call this "extremely powerful" validated me. That was the moment when I knew I was writing a real book that could be meaningful to people other than myself.

I am also grateful to Katie Ramsey for being an early reader. I gained confidence when she told me it deserved to be published because it has the potential to change people's hearts.

I absolutely must thank my editors, Sudi "Rick" Karatas and Stephanie Gunning. I would have never been able to organize this crazy life and put it onto paper without their patience and kindness and perseverance.

In the final three years of writing my memoir, Rick helped me immensely. He took my written recollections and helped me organize and flesh them out into chapters, always allowing me to work at my own pace.

My production manager and copy editor, Stephanie, is an angel. She earned her wings working with me. The best thing about working with her was having faith in her professionalism and knowing that my life story would be safe in her hands. Writing a memoir about a difficult past is a vulnerable experience. She understood my message right off the bat and I knew she would help me express it as intended.

After painting the artwork for the cover, I left it in Dan Khoury's capable hands at Digital Imagining Specialists in Santa Monica, California. He scanned it photographically so that it would be printable. Graphic designer Gus Yoo then took it and prepared the final cover. I am grateful to them both for helping me present my writing in a beautiful package.

I am grateful to Craig MacLeod for the photos of me, and to Najat Washington for her work on the page layout.

I am absolutely astounded that the universe chose to surround me by the most wonderful and supportive and kind and loving people that have never once let me down. Sharing this human experience with this extremely special circle has been something I will cherish for all of eternity! And I hope to see you all in the next life or whatever comes next!

FOREWORD

Samantha Cotton

My uncle Cody has always seemed superhuman to me—beautiful, strong, and all-knowing. As an adult, I know now that he wasn't built that way by accident.

If anyone has a story to tell it's him. Instead of letting himself become a victim, he shattered glass, breaking away from what was expected of him more than once, and made his own happy ending.

Cody's story is one that inspires hope in us to go after what we want, to take what the world throws at us and throw it right back, and to never settle.

If you're looking for a little inspiration, proof that you can change your stars, this is it.

INTRODUCTION

My name at birth was Patrick Cody Dennis, and this is my memoir. I have only lived forty-four short years, but oh so much has happened. I'm here to tell my story for all of those who have suffered in one way or another. I'll share the details of many of my personal broken and shattered moments, as these led me to develop beautiful scars that are my strengths today. Let me share these with you. They can be your strengths too because we are ALL in this life together. Without our scars, we are just blind drifters drifting aimlessly through wasted lives.

I choose to look at the years of violence I endured in my childhood and teens as beautiful gifts. Your scars and your pain also can become your personal gifts and strengths, which, in turn, can help others. The actual actions in terrible moments in your life may or may not have been your choice. But what you do with those moments is absolutely your choice.

Let the following pages show you what I mean.

When I decided I needed to tell my story, I knew that I would have to go places in my mind that I'd left behind long ago—to painful memories I had tucked away inside and only visited in random moments. If you've ever experienced violence or emotional trauma, perhaps you know what I mean. When a smell, a picture in a magazine, or something that a mother says to her child in the checkout line brings you back to those places, your memory presents them to you to relive. That color, smell, or sound could be so fleeting, and yet, in that brief moment, wherever you are, it seems familiar. There is a slight nausea, and then it's gone. Your subconscious protects you by carrying the painful memory safely away.

If you're reading this book and find yourself revisiting your own dark places, especially those you thought were buried long ago, I hope in that moment you know that you're not alone, and that others, like me, have learned how to survive. Maybe, by understanding the ways I did, you can too.

I'll start from the beginning and speak as bluntly as I can from start to finish because I know no other way to be. I hope my journey can help you on your journey. We all have a story and here's mine.

CHAPTER ONE

The Stars Align
How the Family Cycle
of Abuse Started

"It is not in the stars to hold our destiny,
but in ourselves."

—WILLIAM SHAKESPEARE

Family History

My mother's mother had three children, my mother and her two older brothers. She left her three very young kids with their father, a man she had to have known was a very bad person. I've always wondered what made my grandma, Patricia, whom I was named after and never met, leave her helpless two-year-old girl and two little boys with this monster. I can only speculate that she felt she had to escape. Even so, I could never wrap my mind around the fact that when she escaped she left her babies behind. She just took off running and never looked back.

My grandfather and his brother, my great uncle, were sexual predators. They had sex with my mother from the time of her earliest memories until her teenage years. Many years afterward, I got her to open up to me and she told me everything. By then, I was in my late thirties and she agreed to stay with me for a couple of months.

During that visit, we spent many nights sitting on the back porch of my beautiful farmhouse in the Ozark Mountains of northwest Arkansas talking about all we had each been through. She told me that her father and uncle had raped her repeatedly throughout her childhood, and for a long time had thought she was in love with her father. Having experienced this specific type of abuse, my mother had inadvertently been taught that violation, sex, and violent abuse were synonymous with love. She unknowingly carried that mindset with her throughout the rest of her life.

I asked her how she was able to cope with the abuse and if she had understood that it was abuse. She told me she eventually learned to like it from her father because her dad didn't make it hurt like her uncle did. She seemed very upset that her uncle had done it to her, but then showed a very different face when she spoke of her own father committing this heinous act. When I asked her why, she simply replied, "Because my daddy didn't make it hurt."

That is all I need to say about my mother's childhood. It sickens me to my core even to write this much, so I'll move on. Although it is very sad to learn of my family background, please stay with me. I promise we will together find a beautiful ending to this wild story, and I *will* leave you with a beautiful gift as well. I just have to get through the telling of this horrid nightmare to get to the really beautiful things.

Mom

When my siblings and I were taken from our mother, social services would describe our mother as: "A pretty woman with a very unstable personality. She can be calm, kind, and quiet one minute, and then get very loud, vicious, and violent the next. She uses and abuses narcotics and alcohol. She has had many addresses and live-in boyfriends. She is extremely neglectful of her children, extremely abusive, and horribly inappropriate as a mother figure. She has a low level of intelligence and never completed high school. She didn't work while she had the children and was on welfare and food stamps."

My mother was seventeen when she met my father, a handsome truck driver ten years her senior. He was charming and just enough years ahead of her to supplement her obviously fully ingrained and inevitable daddy issues. They began a family that included my two older sisters and myself. My mother gave birth to my oldest sister, Nina, at age nineteen, then to Sue at twenty-one, and me at age twenty-four. All seemed to be going well enough until the damage from her childhood forced its way to the surface. That was when she decided that my father's truck driving schedule took him away too much to fulfill her needs. Remember, she had been raised to mistake sex and abuse for love. She slept with our father's friends and whomever else was present in an attempt to fill a void she didn't even know she had.

One night, our dad came home from a long truck-driving job and found our mother having sex with his best friend. She ended up leaving us behind with our dad and just taking off. I was four months old at the time. Our father moved us to the home of his family in another town in Texas a couple hours away so they could help him take care of us. Six months later, when a babysitter was alone with us at the house, Mom came and took us away from there.

We did not hear from our father again. We heard later that he remarried soon after he and our mother split, and he was living somewhere in northern Texas.

Because our mother had no plan whatsoever, she found herself and her children homeless, aimless, and starving.

When we were living on the streets, my mom was still searching for the love that she could never find because everything she knew and had been taught about love came from a disturbed and disgusting man who knew absolutely nothing of love at all. Her constant search for love took our mother far away from us kids more often than not. It did not include us. I know she loved us the best way she knew how, but it just wasn't enough. Her abused childhood did not give her a blank check to neglect her own children.

If that remark sounds like resentment, I promise you it's not. I forgave my mother a very long time ago and made a conscious choice not to carry that bitter poison with me for the rest of my life. Our mother's time away from us grew longer as months went by. Sometimes she would be gone for days or even weeks. My two older sisters and I suddenly found ourselves in a life where we roamed daily, searching for anything that resembled food, and when night fell, any shelter would do.

My mother became desperate, and as a last resort ended up trading sex for food, drugs, or alcohol. In her mind, she was also receiving love. "Love" from these strangers was enough to put food in our bellies and sometimes a roof over our head. As most everyone knows, what she was receiving from the strangers was not love at all. It couldn't possibly replace the attention she had received from her father and certainly not the real love that she received from my father, which she ultimately rejected because it wasn't love as she thought it was supposed to be. Because of the new situation she herself created, she found herself addicted to many drugs. This was the 1970s when drugs were even more prevalent than they are today and not understood to be as harmful as we now know they are.

My mom left the three of us under bridges and in abandoned and broken-down cabins in the woods, anywhere that resembled a shelter. She would always promise to return in a few hours, and I believe she always meant to, but then she would go and get so drunk or high that she would just forget where she left us. My two older sisters had to feed all three of us.

Later, my mom had two more babies, my younger brothers. She had briefly fallen for a man and had his child, and then he was sent to prison. She then fell for his brother and had his child and then he went to prison too before his son was born. As a result, I have two younger brothers who are each other's cousins as well as brothers.

We were now five kids being raised by a drug-addicted prostitute on a never-ending quest for a certain kind of love that could never be found.

Sometimes Mom would forget we were her children. In her drug-diluted state of mind, she saw us as her competition. She didn't realize that the men whose company she kept were molesting and raping her small children—who were left defenseless when she inevitably passed out. Yes, the cycle of abuse was repeating.

Mom finally had enough wits to see what was happening, but instead of protecting her children decided she would trade our purity for drugs and money.

In 1980, my mother agreed to carry a baby as a surrogate for some friends in exchange for a car. She was literally going to trade the unborn child for a car! After she had a miscarriage, she was upset when they told her they wouldn't give her the car. That was her third miscarriage due to drug and alcohol abuse. By that point, Mom was losing a battle she wasn't even fighting.

Despite my mom's overwhelming shortcomings, zero awareness, and lack of any intention to be better, there were good times too. I remember my mother singing "Pretty Woman" and "Heartache Tonight" into a hairbrush and watching her dance around the kitchen. We were staying at a house out in the woods that had been abandoned. When she was in a good mood, it was mesmerizing and contagious. Her joy was like a wave lifting us up and a "family karaoke session" ensued in whatever place had briefly become our home.

But then something would always change, and her mood would turn inside out. It was like a switch had flipped. The light in her eyes would darken for no reason and without warning. Her growing and irrational dark wave would soon crest and crash over us and the happy moment would be gone.

We knew we weren't safe from this part of our mother, so we would hide.

Our mother always had a childlike spirit. My sister Sue told me that when I was a baby and we all lived together as a family they would have surprise water balloon fights inside the house, and they loved to wake our dad up this way. Our mother enjoyed singing to us and taking us to the lake to swim and fish. She could be really fun until anything or nothing would make her into an unstable, cruel, and violent person. When she was drunk, she became a vicious being. Anyone could see the flash in her eyes and face as she changed from bright to dark within seconds.

Any number of things could happen in moments like these, like a backhand across the face that would send one of us flying across the floor. Or she'd grab our hair and get her face really close to ours and say the most ugly and hateful things in a low growl in her best, very successful attempt to sound evil.

Over time, she allowed the alcohol she drank to absolutely consume her, and in turn, consume us kids. This was an enormous problem that rapidly grew bigger and was constantly becoming more severe. So those happy times became fewer and far between.

Sometimes after Nina and Sue would get us boys off to bed, they would keep watch at the door in case Mom came home in a drunken rage. Many times, they found her drunk and passed out in the front yard. One time when they looked out, she was laying naked in the yard and several men were taking turns with her. My sisters had to run outside and push them off of her while simultaneously trying to get her to wake up and come into the house. When they got her inside and poured water on her to wake her up, she beat them for waking her. Directly afterwards, she went back to being sweet as honey, like nothing had ever happened.

CHAPTER TWO

On the Road Again with Mom

"Maybe home is somewhere I'm going and have never been before."
—WARSAN SHIRE

We were going from one place to another with our mom. We were constantly on the road, either walking next to it or riding in a stranger's car. My mom loved to hitchhike, partly because she liked the attention she would get from men because she was beautiful. To her, this attention also meant love. While she was trying to pick up a guy on the road, she would have us children hide in a ditch or behind a building. She always managed to get someone to stop; then she would explain that she also had kids with her, and she could pay the man with sex once we got back to his place. Sometimes these cars just drove off but other times she would turn and give us the signal that it was okay to come out and we would run out of our hiding spot and get in the car with her.

I remember walking along a very long bridge once. We were supposed to hold hands and walk in a row, like baby ducks, because our mother was afraid that one of us would fall off the bridge. A very motherly thing to do, I think! My mother turned around halfway across the bridge and saw that I had let go of my sister's hand. Right there, she beat me so violently that I fell to the ground on the edge of the bridge. Then she started kicking me in the leg, and it hurt so much it took me a long time to stand up again. My sister Sue helped me up, and I limped the rest of the way across that bridge wondering how long it would be until the familiar bruises would show up. I felt the swelling in my elbow grow but kept my head held high, because even though I was a small child, life had already turned me into a very tough kid. I still had my pride and cars were driving past us, and I didn't want them to see my pain.

I had a recurring nightmare after that that lasted throughout the rest of my childhood. In the dream, I was endlessly falling off a bridge with my siblings all hand in hand. Our mother wasn't with us.

Another extremely memorable hitchhiking ride was the time a guy picked us up in an old, ugly 1960's boat of a car. We had all piled in as usual, but this time I was told to sit up front. I always liked to land in the backseat with my siblings because that's where the fun was. For some reason, however, I was now in the passenger's seat and my mom was in the middle. As I breathed in the familiar scent of the damp night air mixing with cigarette smoke, I watched all of the bright business signs pass us by. The windows were rolled down and the breeze felt amazing. I sat on my bent knees so I could let the wind blow into my hair and over my face. I became thirsty and told my mom that several times, thinking she couldn't hear me with the windows down. She finally got annoyed, as most mothers do when their child repeats the same demand over and over, so she whipped her head around and shouted for me to drink some of this random guy's grape soda. I didn't know him, and he appeared to be a very dirty man with a big, dirty beard surrounding the cigarette hanging from his mouth. He was a complete stranger to us all, so I refused to drink after him.

Even though we already had eaten many meals from the trash and leftover meals that were handed to us by kind strangers, I just didn't want to drink from the same can as this very scary-looking man who was already too close for comfort. My mom kept insisting but I wouldn't budge, which ignited mom's familiar rage. She was still slapping the crap out of me when the stranger in the driver's seat asked her to stop.

I stood my ground even though the strikes became harder with each blow until finally she forced me to drink it. Around the rim of the can were chunks of chewed-up peanuts that had escaped his mouth with the backwash and I had to drink those too. Those tiny peanut pieces really stuck inside my mouth and some bits were trapped between my teeth and gums. To this day, I can't drink after people and I will not eat peanuts.

Temporary Homes

Our homes ranged from old warehouses and abandoned cabins on the sides of nameless country roads to a cardboard slat under a bridge overpass. In whatever home we claimed, you would find my mother in the wildest places around it, searching for flowers to fill an old coffee can or anything that could be used as a vase. Once, this was an old Folgers coffee can that she spotted sticking out of the ground that had orange rust and red and yellow colors swirling around the outside. She would collect flowers, place them in the coffee can or whatever she found and bring them to wherever we were. This would become the centerpiece for our new home that would last for one night, a few days, or sometimes weeks.

Our home was not defined by where we were staying or the number of rooms in it, or by a yard or even walls— sometimes a home didn't even have those. Wherever we were, it was home because we were together.

Mom would do things like she did with the coffee can and other things to create beauty in our homes. She would find colorful stones and bits of shiny broken glass that had caught her eye, and glue these to the outside of cigarette packs and cartons to decorate our new living space. This was her way of trying to help us all escape from the horrible life she created for us. By decorating and trying to make things look pretty, she went to a happy place in her mind and she wanted us to go to that place with her. This was the only indication ever offered that she was aware that our lives needed any improvement, or we needed some sort of escape, no matter how small. This was one of the few things she did that was motherly.

Really, she was the one we needed to escape. Although I do believe that seeing those beautiful wildflowers in contrast to that dirty, old coffee can was one of the first things that ever taught me how to truly see the beauty in what might seem like nothing at all.

This gift alone may be the only reason I never gave up seeking beauty in the world.

This tiny act has been carried with me throughout my life and I believe it may be the greatest gift my mother ever gave me.

My mother would leave, and we children would play outside until it got dark or too cold. When she returned, we would eat whatever food she had managed to scrounge up for us seated around the can of flowers.

We stayed in more places than I can count. Here are two that stand out most in my memory.

Our Home Under a Bridge

We were traveling somewhere between Texas and Arkansas. On our way, we spent about a week living under a bridge with big concrete ramps that led to the protective underside of the bridge's ledge, where no one could see us. Mom had us kids clean off the spider webs and dirt daubers' nests while she fashioned a bed out of flattened cardboard boxes. After we were all set up, she inevitably left us with very strict instructions to stay hidden and not to go down the ramp toward the street, saying she would be back soon. We stuck to the rules for probably a day. Then, as children do, we became bored and took that cardboard bed and slid down the ramp toward the traffic. It was like sledding, but without snow. We had fun doing that over and over and it just felt like an amazing adventure and the biggest slide I had ever seen.

We had blankets and not much else at that point. We also weren't the only people who lived there. Three other groups lived under the same bridge and their fires kept us warm at night, but my sisters made it very clear that no one else was to come to the section that we had carved out as our home.

My mom would leave each day and always planned to come back at night and then would party and get high and forget where she left us. My sister Sue would have to go out and find food for us, sometimes from a dumpster and sometimes just from a nice person who took pity on her.

Nina, the oldest, couldn't help that much because she had eye surgery when we were little, and her eyesight was minimal at times. Her task, therefore, was staying behind to look after us boys.

We didn't really know what was happening. We just always had a sense that we had a destination, but we just didn't really know what or where that was. And I always felt that we were very far from it. So, we just assumed we were on an adventure.

Any time on any day my mother could show up and tell us that it was time to move on.

Our Honkytonk Home

One of our many temporary homes was a *honkytonk*, as our mother called it—a tavern where she sang. This was literally the only job I ever knew her to have while we lived with her. At that time, there were only four of us. Randy was still a baby. There was an apartment above the pub that had a steep staircase on the outside of the building which you had to climb to get to. We stayed up there for what seemed like ages with some men and our mother.

The mattress we slept on upstairs only had a little fabric left and it was stretched across some exposed metal springs. We had to sleep on one side of it, so we didn't fall between the springs.

I liked it much better when we would stay downstairs with our mother while she worked at night. We couldn't stay in the apartment when she wasn't there, as it belonged to one of those men—though I don't know which one—and he wouldn't allow it.

Downstairs, we would all fall asleep underneath one of the booths towards the back by the long hallway that led to the restrooms. Sometimes I peeked out of our tiny hideaway and I loved the way the lights from the jukebox lit up the gently moving layers of smoke that hovered in the air with all of those beautiful colors. The whole room looked like it was enchanted.

I felt comfortable and safe under that table in our booth next to my little brother—safe in our nest on the floor. My two older sisters were protectively perched above us on red vinyl benches. We always had our little blankets that our mother carried with her. We stayed there until my mother was done with whatever she was doing and told us it was time for us all to retreat to the metal mattress in the very dark and dirty apartment upstairs.

CHAPTER THREE

Ghost Stories

Some memories haunt me, and then there are some
memories that are haunted.

Mom had an instinctual knack for finding old places that time had passed by. We'd be walking down the highway and suddenly take off down some little dirt road with a tall line of weeds running down the middle that most people drive right past and never even notice. To be fair, it was probably easier for us to spot these places since we were on foot. We would pause and wait for a long break in the already scarce traffic, and then, at the right moment, scurry off into the woods so that no one would be alarmed by a woman and her kids disappearing into the wilderness.

At the end of the always overgrown and abandoned driveways we were traveling, there would surely be some broken-down cabin or abandoned house in which to shelter. One of the biggest ones we stayed at was in Texas when I was about three. It was so ramshackle that it didn't even have a roof over most of it anymore.

The only part that did have a roof was a very small kitchen in the back that was not even big enough for us all to sleep in. Because the roof had caved in over most of the house, we found ourselves occupying what must have been the living room at some point. We all had to pack into one dry corner of the room. On one wall was a huge picture window that had no glass in it. There was no electricity and no water.

We had our usual blankets with us to make a sleeping pallet on the floor. We brought these blankets everywhere. I remember specifically how my mother would make this bed every night for us no matter where we were. We would all stand back as she would straighten out all the blankets on the floor. When she was done, she would give us a signal to pile in. Many times, I waited and watched her do this, using the very last of my energy to stand and wobble long enough for her to complete the task before collapsing. We would all cuddle up with her and each other, feeling so cozy and hopeful that this would be one of the nights that she didn't leave—and then she would disappear.

One night, not long after we had fallen asleep, an enormous and powerful storm woke us. The trees in the woods surrounding our house were whistling loudly as the wind forced its way through their branches. The rain was being blown so intensely that it looked like it was coming horizontally into our shell of a building. We just huddled together in awe of its ferocity as we watched the flashes of lightning and waited for chasing claps of thunder. Rain showered in through the huge, open window that was only a few feet away from the safe, dry island of our corner. To many kids, this probably would have been a traumatic experience, but not us. We had spent many nights alone, even weeks, and confronted similar situations. To me, it was just another kind of an adventure—at least at the beginning.

As the storm raged, the flooding around the house became obvious and pushed us beyond our comfort level. The storm seemed to have no intention of fading anytime soon, so we actually began to be uncharacteristically afraid. As I felt my sisters' fear climbing higher, mine followed. We were trying to be brave, but the storm was getting the best of us; and we began to panic as it became clear that there was nowhere to escape to. Then we all noticed a slowly increasing glow coming from the direction of the tiny kitchen. As the glow grew, the storm seemed to get quieter—or at least we didn't notice it anymore. All I knew in that moment was that I was okay, and my siblings were okay, and that was all that mattered. The glowing turned into more of a sensation of kindness and love that I felt and heard in the depths of my soul.

In a shocking moment, a beautiful lady in a magical light blue dress that seemed to be dancing or floating around her on its own emerged from the kitchen and came towards us in our den. We had absolutely no idea where she came from but a voice in my head said I knew. She had been cooking in the kitchen and brought us food. Or at least the kitchen was where she brought the food to us from. An immense amount of warmth and love that I had never known before and (I'm not quite sure I have ever felt since) flowed through me. The food smelled incredibly delicious, especially for a hungry tiny tummy like mine.

The lady sat down beside our pallet and we all began to eat. I was only four, so it didn't occur to me how absurd it was that someone was here cooking for us in the middle of nowhere—and in the middle of a storm. She didn't speak out loud to us, but we were all sort of communicating or having an exchange of thoughts with this beautiful stranger who seemed so familiar.

Still feeling her beautiful energy, I was suddenly aware that the storm had continued raging around us. I looked over at the huge window with no glass that had been letting in all of the rain previously and it was now shielding us from the rain and wind as if glass had somehow been installed at that moment. The skeleton of walls seemed somehow solid and secure and the sound of the storm was now muffled in my ears and mind. I was suddenly aware that the only thing that filled the space was kindness.

To this day, I don't know if this woman was human. Was she a spirit? A ghost? An angel? Does it matter who she was or where she came from? In our time of need, she was everything. And the inaudible language she was speaking was unmistakably love in its purest form.

The next morning, we woke up and everything was dry. The sun was out, so we just started playing. I climbed out of the big picture window that was again vacant with no glass. I wandered and explored around the new site and found a little windup toy in the dirt, it was R2-D2, the little round robot from *Star Wars!* I washed off my new toy in a mud puddle left behind by the storm, the whole while thinking, *Holy crap, I have a toy that actually works and isn't broken!* After I washed mud out of all its little parts using the water in a mud puddle, that dirty little wind-up robot became the newest, shiniest toy I had ever seen!

The Haunted Tombstone

At the edge of the woods behind one of the random houses we stayed in, there was an old tombstone that was mossy and tilted. You couldn't quite see the stone from the backyard. You had to step into the woods a few feet. My sister Nina told me the stone was put there for a young girl. My sisters and I would frequently talk around it like we were talking to this girl. We spoke of her and to her like she was standing right in front of us. We were huddled around and talking to nobody yet having a full conversation.

I never saw her, but Sue and Nina seemed to know exactly whom we were talking to in detail and to have become friends with this invisible person. They both even knew the girl's name. We would stand around and chat with her for hours. I was always a little too on edge about it all to contribute much to these conversations.

We told our mom about the girl several times and she just dismissed it. I think she thought we were just playing or pretending. I was confused as to why she was not more concerned or wouldn't want to meet the girl that her kids were spending hours in the backyard with.

The last time we walked through the backyard to the edge of the woods to the tombstone to talk to the girl, my oldest sister, Nina, was mad at her for some reason unbeknownst to me. While Sue tried to calm her down, Nina threw a short, intense fit and finally kicked the tombstone in an explosion of rage!

All three of us seemed to know instantly that this had been a very, very bad thing to do because we all spun on our heels and walked back to the house very quickly, acting scared. A growing and heavy darkness was extremely obvious, so we walked hand in hand not looking back no matter what. Back at the house, we separated and went about our own schedules, trying to put the possible repercussions of the kick out of our thoughts and trying to downplay its significance somehow in our minds.

I started riding my tricycle back and forth on the sidewalk in the front of the house, keeping in bounds of a zone from which I could not see the tombstone that was set slightly back into the tree line. Back and forth I went, again and again, with my fear beginning to slowly grow. Then, all at once, I heard my sisters screaming from inside the house and the entire house coming alive with sounds of terror. I frantically abandoned my oversized tricycle, knocking it over into the grass, then almost tripped over it in my haste to go to my family's aid.

As I got to the front door, my mom came running out with my two brothers in her arms and my sisters following right behind her. She almost knocked me over. I looked beyond my family and saw that everything in the house, including dishes, pillows, couch cushions, a vase, and some kind of a plastic swan planter, was floating about four feet off the ground. According to my sister, something flew into the mirror attached to the dresser, breaking it, just before everything else levitated.

Mom yelled to me, "C'mon, Coat Hanger," which was my nickname, and frantically gestured for me to move quickly with her. I got this nickname from my mom because as a kid I would always look for these wire coat hangers. I would put them on my head and bend the hook or corners up. After I reshaped them I would wear them proudly! I had several I had bent to perfection and at night I arranged them into a line next to wherever I was sleeping so they would be there again for me in the morning. I just thought they were some kind of space age hat or antenna. If I didn't have one on my head at the time then I would have a little red mark across my forehead from having recently worn one and taken it off. My young and creative mind sprouted from a coat hanger hat. As far as nicknames go, I imagine this one had some room for improvement, but anytime I heard my new name I would swell with pride.

I turned around and looked in the direction of my tricycle, which was where I left it. I saw that in the fleeting moments of my absence, it had been buried in dirt. The only thing sticking out of the earth was the handlebars. The dirt around it seemed undisturbed and all that existed was a nice, even patch of grass.

Of course, I did not want to leave my tricycle! We all took turns trying to pull it out of the ground for a brief moment and then decided it wasn't worth it to stay, as the place was too scary. We left that haunted house quickly, never looked back, and took nothing with us.

Another time—I don't remember where we were exactly—my sisters and my mom were sitting at the foot of the bed on the floor watching a movie on a big TV that was built into a big wooden consul, as most were in the early 1980s. *Alice in Wonderland* was the movie. My two little brothers were next to me, asleep on the side of the bed. I was in the middle. I watched as Alice fell down the rabbit hole and thought she was going to hell. The idea that hell was at the center of the earth made enough sense to me. She kept falling and falling, so hell was the obvious conclusion of my four-year-old mind.

I could see the top of my mom's head and my two sisters next to her as I began to doze off. All of a sudden, a sheet came over me and my sleeping brothers! I heard Mom and my sisters screaming. The sheet was smashing my face so I couldn't talk, and my lips were fighting to keep it out of my mouth. Sue told me afterward that when they first turned around (before the screaming commenced) they could hear me trying to speak. The sheet looked like it had shrunk and was vacuum-sealed onto us boys. My sisters were trying to pull it off and having no success. They said it looked like the sheet was trying to suffocate us. But despite the danger, my brothers didn't wake up throughout the entire experience.

My mom said she had heard a loud thumping, like a huge drum, from the other room. At first she thought it was a truck in the distance. Then it kept getting louder and louder and was getting closer by the second. Eventually, the deafening sound filled the room and the walls seemed to expand and contract as if they were breathing. Finally, the sheet released itself and became limp again in an instant. Once we were free, my mother grabbed all of us kids and ran in the direction away from the growing and thunderous sound and we escaped out the nearest window. Once again we left everything, even though we still had very little.

CHAPTER FOUR

Abuse

"Never wish them pain. That's not who you are. If they caused your pain, they must have pain inside. Wish them healing. That's what they need."

—NAJWA ZEBIAN

A Very Rude Awakening

We found ourselves in another random trailer home. I was three or four years old and asleep in one of the back rooms with my siblings when I awoke to the sound of footsteps coming down the hall. My mom came into the room and pulled me out of bed. She sounded like she was trying to be quiet and gentle, but all her actions were quite the opposite. She was stumbling and obviously on some kind of drug or drunk or both. She brought me out of the quiet room alone and led me down the long hallway toward some noise.

I was wearing a grown man's white undershirt as pajamas since I had none of my own. As she walked,

27

she was pulling me faster than I wanted to walk. My eyes were still adjusting to light as I had been sound asleep just moments before. When we reached the living room, I saw a lot of people there sitting on several couches. A coffee table in the middle of the room was covered with glasses, bottles, and overflowing ashtrays. The music was playing so loudly I could barely hear. I was immediately embarrassed because I became extremely aware that I was dressed only in a super-long man's tee-shirt, now front and center among all these strangers. The room was full of people that were not there when I went to sleep.

Mom sat down on the couch next to this guy I remember liking because he had been really nice to me earlier in the day. We hung out like we were best friends. He and my mother began to try to convince me to do something, although I wasn't quite sure what it was. I was confused and then my mother took my hand and put a marijuana joint in it. I obviously had no idea what this thing was. She then began to instruct me on how to breathe in its smoke. This went against all of my basic instincts and I tried to push back. I wasn't quite sure what was happening, but I could tell from the vibe in the room that I did not want any part of it.

The crowd of people were getting really riled up about the idea of me smoking the joint and all of them were trying to tell me it was okay to do it. Despite my reluctance, they finally just put it to my mouth and forced me to breathe. I was coughing and coughing and coughing. Either they spun me or the room itself began to spin. I was so confused as I smelled the smoke and began choking, feeling like my mouth was too dry to talk. And no matter how badly I wanted to cry or run, I couldn't escape.

My mother and the guy I thought was safe earlier that day were now laughing hysterically and I became terrified. I still couldn't breathe, and I remember wondering why that guy was laughing. The damage was in their laughter. I felt betrayed though I didn't know why until many years later.

Then again, the person who was laughing there with her new boyfriend that night wasn't the mother I knew—not really. The woman I saw that night was unrecognizable because I had never seen that side of her until then. That's the side of her that always kept her away from us. That's the side of her that made her forget that she had children and where she put them. That's the side she used when she was out with her friends for days and would forget everything that had ever happened. That's the side of her that eventually got all five of us taken away from her.

The way she acted was partly a result of the drugs and alcohol. Also, it was because she was a product of a similar childhood as the one we were having.

This was just part of the cycle of damage in our family.

My memory of this incident ends abruptly. Because I don't remember going to sleep, I'm guessing I passed out. The next day, I felt horrified and extremely betrayed by my mom (more than usual) and this guy.

The next morning there were a couple of people sleeping on the couch, others outside that had not been to bed yet, and a couple more people were asleep in the grass. They were all scattered around the yard doing something.

When the new guy friend of my mother saw me standing in the doorway of the trailer, he ran up to me like nothing was wrong and we were still pals. He took my hand and pulled me to the edge of the yard by a flowing drainage ditch and showed me a very big turtle. I was really excited because I thought maybe it was going to be my pet until he stepped back and ripped the shell off of it to show me there were eggs inside it.

This violent act sent my mind and my heart into a spiral of thought that this was indeed the reality of my life, and I was never going to be safe around any grownup. The first man that I thought was safe had just shown me another sinister and cruel side of humanity that I had not seen before.

This just shows you the screwed up mindset of these people we were around.

The Darkest Night

There would be times, between our many homes, when we would go stay with one of our mother's new boyfriends or just the "boy of the night." Often we'd find ourselves in a broken-down trailer home with thick, dirty, smokey air and too much stained furniture.

There were always a lot of people around and a loud, drug-filled party going on while my siblings and I slept in some corner of the house. The inside of these places often smelled like cigarettes and old mold, and the carpet would make you itch if you lay on it for too long.

I would always wake up with a stuffy nose after being in one of these places until I adapted. Then the runny nose would stop.

There was a long list of places like this where we stayed on our travels from southern Texas to Little Rock, Arkansas.

One time, a very tall, redheaded man made his way into the living room where all five of us were asleep in our usual blanket palette on the floor. Sue and I were in the middle, as we kids usually slept in birth order. The party must have been elsewhere on this particular night because the trailer was quiet and our mother was passed out in a room at the end of a very long, dark hallway. Sue and I grabbed each other's hands when we heard him walking slowly, breathing heavily, and stumbling down the hall. We faked sleep as he made it to our end, then paused and surveyed the room. We knew what was about to happen.

The man looked over us, perusing us before choosing who would be his victim. We peeked at him, still motionless, every now and then to see what he was doing. He made his way slowly toward us and held onto a wall or piece of furniture every chance he got. He finally stopped at our feet and looked down at us for just a moment longer. There was then the sound of his belt unbuckling and his pants slipping down.

I can still remember the sound that his heavy belt and buckle made, a clank and thud, as they hit the floor around his ankles and by our feet. The sound of the weak trailer home floor creaking under the added thud from the weight of him falling to his knees. The smell of him and his breath that I would like to forget but will never be able to, merging and becoming one with the dank smell of the old house.

The look on Sue's face was burned into my memory as she was dragged by her ankles underneath the covers while trying to keep them tightly shut and at the same time trying to keep her sight on me. I squeezed her hand tightly and had no intention of ever letting go. Her head was just above the blanket looking at me through squinted blue eyes. I held her hand (but made sure the guy didn't see out of the fear he would take her into another room) and I listened to the nothing.

I think my mind has blocked out the obvious sounds the huge, redheaded man at our feet must have made because I don't remember anything else after that. I was only focused on being there as strongly as I possibly could be for my sister. Sue never made a sound and didn't struggle at all as he raped her. Hers was the bravest face I have ever seen in my life. I knew she was crying quietly because the portion of the pillow that her head was still resting on was slowly becoming soaked with her tears.

This silent bravery was a textbook response to the horror for us, something that we had learned to do from a young age. If we struggled or made noise, it would make the monsters more violent. You see, when people are doing something wrong they kind of go into a place where they are hidden. In the darkness is where they tend to do the most damage. For someone like this, just to be seen is to be exposed as the monster that they are.

A child's innocence is the brightest light in that darkness and shines an unbearable light on the person doing the wrong. When someone is caught doing something wrong they usually go into a defense mode and lash out in a distraction of violence. This is why, when those men were doing what they did, they would become enraged if they saw us looking at them or seeing them at all.

The contrast of my innocence and Sue's would have been like a mirror of guilt for the man and he would not have liked what he saw and would have become enraged. So, we kept our eyes shut tightly so as to not make the situation worse.

I looked at a vase on a shelf and tried to plan for how I could get to it and back to knock this man out, all the while knowing it was probably impossible, nonetheless trying to convince myself that I could do it. Really, I could do nothing. I was helpless to combat an adult. I was only four years old.

When he was done and had slithered away, we lay there in the dark in the quiet aftermath. There was my sister's face, still crying silently from the edge of the blanket. Her hand was sweaty in mine and I squeezed it as hard as I could, until my knuckles turned white, just so she would know she wasn't alone.

This wasn't the first time that something like this had happened to one of us and we knew it wouldn't be the last. After the horrible man left, we huddled together in the dark and finally fell back asleep hand in hand. And I can promise you that I have not let go of my sister's hand since that day. We are very, very close.

My sisters told my mother several times about these men, hoping that she would come to our defense somehow and end this nightmare. When she actually would acknowledge what my sisters were telling her, she would just get enraged, call them sluts, and accuse them of trying to steal her boyfriends. They were seven and eight years old.

I think, because my mom enjoyed having sex with her dad that she thought her daughters liked it too— and therein lies the cycle of generational abuse!

Pay close attention. You may be in a cycle of some kind yourself and don't even know it. More than likely, your family cycle's not as intense as this cycle but that is, of course, relative.

If you are in a cycle worse than this, then it may be more obvious to you.

Maybe our mother was like that because she didn't understand that things like that were truly wrong because of what she had gone through as a child and had been programmed to think. I'm not sure that she had ever learned right from wrong. I could do nothing to protect my sisters. I'd never felt or would ever feel as helpless as I did on that one horrible night.

Later, the social service case file would say that Sue and Nina had been raped more times than they could count.

Today Sue is one of the most extraordinary people I know. She is a good mother. We have had wonderful times together. We've made wonderful memories. We raised our kids at the same time and had so many happy adventures together. She is proof that one can overcome a horrible situation and live a good life. She is and always will be my greatest hero.

Taken Away from Mom

It was inevitable that we would eventually be taken from my mom. We were living at Uncle Brody's house, the home of our grandfather's nefarious brother. Our mother was there with us and was trying to explain to us that we were going away and would be staying somewhere else for a while until she got on her feet.

My sister Sue has told me that she didn't understand what "getting on your feet" meant. She thought maybe our mother was sick or hurt or something and she was trying to get us all cleaned up and pretty because the police were coming to get us. That Mom had already agreed to put us in someone else's care until she was stable.

She was getting us ready and I was four and stubborn, as most kids that age are. I had recently discovered the vast and free world of paper airplanes! I would make a paper airplane any chance I got out of any type of paper that I could get my hands on. Our mother was trying to get me to pick my enormous collection of paper airplanes up off the floor and I wouldn't budge. So, she went into her violent default mode. She grabbed a stick and started chasing me around the backyard with it, trying to hit me. I didn't dare stop running for an instant because I knew what she was capable of. Nina and Sue were running right behind her and screaming for her to stop while yelling for me to run faster and trying to protect me. That's the moment the police and Department of Human Service workers finally showed up.

The chase came to a very abrupt and awkward stop. The social workers gathered up all the five children and my mom, got us calmed down, and took us inside to sit on the couch. My baby brother Charlie was on Sue's lap. Our mother was squatting on the floor, holding Sue's hand and trying to keep us calm while the DHS worker explained how Mom was going to go elsewhere till she got on her feet.

Sue kept looking at our mother thinking, *What's wrong with her? Just stand up*, not realizing this was an idiomatic expression. She thought if Mom stood up then we wouldn't have to leave.

We truly did not understand that there were other options in the world and safer places to live. All we knew was this one woman. People actually want to stay with what's familiar and do not trust the unknown.

Soon, we all quietly got in the car. Car seats were not mandatory back then, so they piled us all in and handed Sue our baby brother, and just drove us away as we waved at Mom, thinking she was just sick and hurt. We weren't wrong.

They took us to the Rainbow House, which was an emergency receiving shelter for children in North Little Rock, Arkansas. We were actually the first kids to be put into that home. It had just opened and was brand new!

We had visitations with our mother after that, but they were supervised because of her extremely unstable and volatile behavior. We would have scheduled visits at the DHS office to meet her and sometimes she would show up and sometimes she wouldn't. She would usually have a man with her even during visits. The DHS office had a special room for this. In this room, there were several overflowing toy chests. It was rare that we would see so many toys and, as children, of course we wanted to play with them. I don't think we understood that we were there to see her or that it was temporary or really what was going on at all.

Mom would become violent and enraged when we gave the toys more attention than her. At that point, the social workers would have to make her leave or calm her down.

During one of the visitations, my little brother Randy was thirsty, so my mom took him to the water fountain and picked him up so that he could reach it. He took a huge mouthful of the water and turned around and spit it out at her, just being a playful three-year-old. My mother dropped him and continued kicking and beating him until the DHS workers could pull her off of him. Me and my sisters were trying to get her to stop, but even though she was a tiny woman, she was much bigger than us and we were no match for her.

That was the day the visitations ended.

The following list of abuses that occurred under our mother's care, or lack thereof, as the case may be, is from our initial DHS family intake summary. We had endured:

- Physical abuse.
- Malnutrition, leading to failure to thrive syndrome.
- Poor clothing.
- Lack of proper shelter.
- Improper sleeping arrangements.
- Lack of supervision.
- Failure to attend school regularly.
- Exploitation and overwork.
- Exposure to unwholesome or demoralizing circumstances.
- Sexual abuse.

- Emotional abuse and neglect.
- Denial of normal experiences that permit a child to feel loved, wanted, secure, and worthy.

Another form of child abuse was added for the sisters: *premature responsibility*. With the birth of each younger brother, the girls had been given the responsibility of feeding, diapering, clothing him. Then, when their three little brothers were older, they had to chase these hyperactive boys around, trying to keep them in the house and alive. Nina and Sue managed this extraordinary task somehow, even while they (and their brothers) were being subjected to all of the aforementioned abuses.

CHAPTER FIVE

Foster Homes and Group Homes

"Home should be an anchor, a pool in the storm, a refuge, a happy place in which to dwell, a place where we are loved and where we can love."

—MARVIN J. ASHTON

The Gateleys

The Gateleys had been missionaries in Korea for years and years. They were salt of the earth type of people and the house parents at the brand-new, beautiful, wonderful, and safe children's shelter we were brought to. It was dumb luck or something much greater that decided this is where they should put us when we separated from our mother that horrible day at the DHS office. As I've said, we were the first kids taken into the new shelter, all five of us together.

The shelter was great. There were toys everywhere and everyone had his or her own room. The building was made of cylinder blocks constructed in the shape of an octagon. In the center of the building was a large family room with a large table. Above this was the most beautiful skylight. Looking like our own personal window, it seemed to peek directly into heaven.

There also was a bicycle just my size. We had access to food and drinks. And they were building a playground in our backyard that looked exactly like the one at the park! We were in heaven! That backyard might as well have been Disney World.

This place felt like a dream.

At first, I thought this was our new permanent home. I also thought it was just going to be us five. I didn't know more kids would come. Every now and then, however, we'd wake up and there would be another very scared and confused kid or a group of siblings who would be black and blue from being beaten by their parents, sitting there at the breakfast table. The cops had come and taken them in the middle of the night and brought them to this safe place.

Since we were the first kids there and thought of it as our home, we thought of anyone else that was new as a guest or a visitor in our home. It took me a while to realize that we were actually sharing this home with them and that they were not just our guests.

Then-Governor Bill Clinton invited us to the state capitol once! I'm not quite sure why. Maybe it was a PR stunt or maybe he'd just heard about five kids who needed a little extra attention. Anyway, we were at the ornate and oh-so-glorious Capitol building of the great State of Arkansas and damn proud of it, and we had no idea why! At least I didn't. I thought it was a church because I was wearing my church clothes.

My two older and much wiser sisters were acting like they were about to meet Jesus himself, so I knew something big was going down. We all stood outside of a big room waiting for HIM to come out of a meeting. I still didn't understand who he was, but I knew we were waiting on someone very important. And maybe he could fly. When he finally emerged from behind a door, looking so tall, like a big oak tree, they introduced us kids to him. He reached down and scooped me up. I still remember the ride from his ankles to his elbows, which seemed like it took forever. I was so high in the air that I felt like a bird perched on a branch about to take flight.

The governor then started walking down the hall pointing at things: statues and paintings on the walls, ceilings, and floors. His long arm pointed and gave me a short jolt each time. My only concern was how I was going to get down from this arm so high in the air.

The next thing I remember is waving goodbye to him and making our way down the very long stairs and getting into our station wagon to go home to the shelter. My sisters were going on and on saying how they were never, ever, ever going to wash their hands again because the great Governor Bill Clinton shook them, so I decided I wasn't going to either.

I'm still not sure any of us really knew who that man was. We certainly found out more about him a few years later.

Mr. and Mrs. Gateley were very special to us since they were the only kind people we had ever encountered and became very protective of us. I did not view them as house parents, I saw them as *our* parents—the parents we were supposed to have.

Other kids would come and go but we were the first, the originals. And the Gateleys kept up with our progress while we were placed in multiple foster homes. When it didn't work out in a particular foster home, we would come back to this wonderful children's shelter, our home base. Eventually, we would come back and there were different house parents running the home. With each change of staff, we would have to reintroduce ourselves and again present our vibrant personalities.

One of the times we were there, the house parents were Jeff and Kim. They were such good people, both very kind and very happy. The type of people that are always smiling and not in a fake or obnoxious way. They always seemed to want to make sure that we were OK. We went to parks with them and I remember experiencing bright, happy kindness from Jeff. He would pick me up and carry me. I remember his facial hair and accepting his masculine energy as safe whereas men before him had never felt safe to be around. I had only known men to hurt me in one way or another. But Jeff's fatherly energy and kindness mixed together showed me that a man can indeed be kind. This was a very new thought for me: *A man can be kind, caring, and safe.*

That was the kind of man that I wanted to be.

That wonderful man, who was only in my life for the blink of an eye, had so much kindness in him that in an instant he became my subconscious role model for the rest of my life.

You never know what your kindness can do for somebody. Even the smallest amount can be such a powerful gift. Use it on yourself and others as often as possible.

Almost Home

In most homes we were placed in, we instinctively knew beforehand, or were told, that we would not be there long. They were intended to be temporary placements.

Once, we were picked up from the children's shelter and taken on a long drive into the country to meet a new family. I was about five years old. This particular family was not supposed to be a temporary placement because they were actually considering adopting us. All five! Together! This was an extremely lucky break because all we had heard by this point was that social services were trying to separate us. We had already survived so much *together* that our intention was to keep doing so.

Sometimes my siblings and I would make a pact before we went to some placements to misbehave so we wouldn't have to stay. If we had heard something bad about a particular place or the couple whose home it was, something that we didn't like, or if we thought they were going to try to separate us, my sisters would devise a plan and tell the rest of us what we should all do to get sent back to the shelter. Many times, we would just act as wild as possible and that would do the trick. We just had to make sure that our behavior was not worth the paycheck that the couple would receive for taking care of us in their home.

We didn't have a plan this time. We were actually excited about the placement.

This couple was older, in their sixties—honestly, probably too old to be taking care of five children this young and with this much energy, who also had some very creative behavioral issues to contend with since we were basically raised in the wild. The husband was a farmer, or at least he looked exactly like the ones from the storybooks to me, when I saw him working in the field as we drove past him and down the long driveway toward his home.

After we had parked and began unloading the brown paper grocery bags that were our "suitcases," the farmer was making his way through the field to meet us while our social worker was busy ringing the doorbell. We were standing behind her, looking around, and taking in the scene of this big, beautiful farm. A gentle-looking woman finally came around to greet us from the side door of the house.

The farmer made it to us at the same time. He said hello and introduced himself to us, gave the lady a kiss on the cheek, and then returned to his work in the field.

The wife was a nice grandma type. She gave me one of the softest hugs I had ever had and I liked her. She smelled like flowers. My two youngest brothers were the wildest of all of us and they were a big problem in a lot of our placement homes. The thought instantly sprung to my mind that I was hoping with all the might that I had that they would not show that side to these people. Not yet.

We were not feral or bad children; we were just in survival mode.

I thought the place seemed cozy and homey right when I stepped inside. This sweet, new lady showed me to the room where I would be staying with my two little brothers. I set my grocery bag of clothes on the floor, turned around, and walked straight outside. Then I got on a green plastic toy tractor that I had spotted when we first drove up and I peddled it directly out to the field where the older man had resumed his work. I didn't know what he was doing, but it looked like it served a purpose and I wanted to do whatever he was doing out there in that field. I pedaled my new tractor right up next to his like I had just shown up for my first day on the job.

The farmer seemed like a nice, healthy, and safe person to be around. My life thus far had gifted me with a sixth sense about such things. I wasn't used to being around those kinds of men. He seemed wholesome and I felt very drawn to that. Whatever he was doing that day in the field, that's what I wanted to be doing too. He was digging a hole or something and I just stood smashing things with a shovel alongside him (helping to my heart's content) and thought that this man just had to become my new dad.

At this point in my childhood, I did already understand that the whole point of home placements was to find new parents. It only made sense that this man was actually supposed to be my dad and I had finally found him. I could have stayed in that field with him for days.

Eventually, when the sun started going down, he sent me back to the house to wash up for dinner. I hadn't seen my siblings for hours, which was probably the longest I had ever gone without seeing them in my life so far. This place felt like a beautiful dream that I never even knew I should or could dream. I was so happy.

I walked into the house with my happy head held high. But I instantly realized that my sisters were in an extremely different mood than they were when I left them. That meant something heavy must have happened while I was gone and my siblings had decided they didn't want to be there. I wasn't a part of the decision this time since I had spent most of the day with my new dad.

For some reason I didn't know, my brothers and sisters had already decided they didn't like this place and I couldn't imagine what it was. Apparently, in my absence the boys had been extra wild, and my oldest sister had already had one of her usual explosive meltdowns because she really struggled to process her emotions. The nice lady was trying to calm everyone down and being really sweet and gentle about it. I was just a spectator from the table, having my late dinner, when she finally managed to quiet everyone and was now sitting in a chair crocheting or making a quilt or something. The TV was on and my siblings were lying around on the floor watching it. I joined them all on the floor and fell fast asleep.

The room had a very different kind of cozy feel to it. I felt extremely safe and almost normal! This was IT! This was finally our new home. That was the first time I felt that kind of atmosphere. I really wanted to stay there.

At some point I managed to make it into my new bedroom, and I woke up the next morning lying in the softest bed I had ever felt in my life. I slowly made my way into the kitchen all the while inspecting my new pajamas and trying to figure out when and how I'd put them on. When I arrived in the kitchen, the nice lady was there making breakfast quickly and my siblings were around the table actually being very well behaved. All seemed right in the world. But then, within moments, the social worker knocked on the door, and just like that, we were shuffled out of the house and into a van with a brown bag of clothes in our laps. Off we went to another placement.

As long as I live, I'll never forget that man in the field and his lovely wife that just wanted to help us.

I had no idea why my siblings hadn't liked it there until I asked my sister Sue about it recently. She told me that they told us the guy's heart was too weak to handle all five of us. His heart was so stressed by our presence that he had actually had to go to the emergency room that morning.

Sue also told me she and Nina felt the couple were trying to step over them. Sue and Nina had been taking care of us for such a long time that they were kind of "our parents," so it was hard for them to be welcoming to these new "bosses."

Apparently, the sweet lady had told Nina and Sue they didn't need to be the parents, and in fact, needed to stop disciplining and taking care of their younger brothers. She'd said that it was their time just to be kids as well. This message had good intent behind it and was obviously delivered to take some pressure off my sisters and release them to be children with no worries, but my sisters had felt they were being demoted, so to speak. So, Sue and Nina intentionally gave the two youngest boys a lot of sugar from a bowl full of candy that was sitting on the coffee table, knowing it would get them all hyped up. They wanted the boys to misbehave so the couple would not want to keep them.

It worked.

CHAPTER SIX

Corelle Hell

"If you're going through hell, keep going."
—ATTRIBUTED TO WINSTON CHURCHILL

From One Hell to Another

They told us from the very beginning that we weren't going to be adopted by this new family, that it was just a long-term foster care situation. The Corelles were a blended family. Mrs. Corelle had three kids of her own, Ronald, Lyle, and Cal. Mr. Corelle had two kids, Sal and Joel. They had been fostering our baby brother, Chase, who was taken from our mom in the hospital after delivery. Because he was born to an alcoholic, he needed special attention while he was detoxing so that he wouldn't die.

The rest of us were still with our mom at this time. None of us knew that the Corelles had Chase for three months before the State gave him back to her.

A few months after Chase's return to Mom, they took all of us away.

When we pulled up to the Corelles, standing on the front porch was this woman, Mrs. Corelle, who had short, fine, stringy hair. She was not very tall and had a frail physique. She was waving and looked extremely happy to see us. She had a huge smile plastered on her face.

An oddly confident-looking teenage boy named Ronald with thick glasses and a perfect part in his dark hair stood next to her with an equally happy grin on his face.

I remember wondering why the strangers were so happy to see us. I couldn't stop looking at them as I climbed out of the car and tried to size up the house and these strange people on the porch.

We unloaded as usual and went inside while the social worker spoke with Mrs. Corelle on the front porch. She was animated and loud with a high-pitched cackle of a laugh that made her thin body shake. She seemed pleasant enough, but I was still unsure of it all. Something inside me was warning me and causing me to pay attention to every detail that I could. We were all guided past this woman and into the house, gathering in a tight group in the living room.

While we waited for his mother to come in, Ronald showed me how to make funny noises into the window unit air conditioner. He clearly wanted to be buddies. He seemed to have taken an instant liking to me. My siblings had already started wandering around and exploring our new home, but Ronald kept me by his side. I was trying to stay in the living room and as close to the social worker, who was still on the front porch, as possible. She never stepped inside the house.

As the social worker started to leave, Mrs. Corelle walked into the house still cheerfully waving goodbye. When the car was gone and the front door had closed, she turned around to face us, reached into a gold-sequined cigarette case from her pocket and lit up. With the cigarette hanging from her mouth, she changed instantly and completely right before our very eyes. The cheerful expression she had obviously practiced and rehearsed was apparently reserved for the social worker. Her face had grown tight and cold in an instant. It seemed bonier than it had been moments before; her eyes now appeared sunken in and darker.

Mrs. Corelle immediately began barking orders at all the kids, delegating chores with her first breath and skipping any pleasant or otherwise introductions. I wasn't even sure if she knew our names yet. She didn't seem to want us there. I knew with every ounce of my tiny body that something was very, very wrong as I glanced out the front window in hope that maybe the social worker felt this also and would be coming back for us.

We had escaped our mother's whirlwind of abuse and neglect and landed right in the lap of a monster far greater than any of us had ever known. The first couple of weeks living with the Corelles, Mrs. Corelle was cold and uncomfortably distant. I actually preferred for her to be distant because any time she started to come closer to me or my siblings my heart would race, as my fear would grow. I felt it as a burning sensation in my scalp and my ears. This was the protective fight-or-flight mode that my body was offering me, but I had no way of taking advantage of it. I stood as tall as possible and planted my feet whenever I was scared.

She was such a dark force that her own children also seemed frightened of her, as were the several cousins, nieces, and nephews that were visiting the house constantly. I felt slightly lost in what seemed like a very big house as I would move about trying to complete and even understand my chores.

My siblings and I were rarely able to be together and there was an eerie silence because we were not allowed to speak to each other. The most we could do was just to give encouraging looks and whisper quickly, if possible, as we passed each other in the dark rooms and hallways.

As time went by and she became more comfortable showing her true self, Mrs. Corelle's evil seemed to grow and take on a form of its own. On many occasions, my little brother Randy got into trouble, probably for wetting his bed and she would call me into the room where she was yelling at him. Though I was not the one being punished, she took both our heads with both her hands and slammed them together, over and over. When she did this, I felt like it would never end. She was only using my skull to hit his skull.

Sometimes she would just slam his or my head into the wall.

Randy had always been a bedwetter. He couldn't help it. It obviously was a result of huge amounts of stress—which no child should ever be exposed to.

Her solution was to beat him nightly and make him sleep in the bathtub.

She let us know she was ashamed of all of us, but whenever there was company over her personality would shift back into the woman we met in those first fleeting moments on the front porch with the social worker. She didn't want people to know that she despised us, and we knew not to give anyone any ideas that might hint of the fast-growing nightmare at home.

Her voice would become melodious and pleasant when we had guests. Sometimes we would hear her voice being kind and lovely and we realized a guest was in the house and we would all emerge knowing that for a little while we were safe.

If it turned out that people were not in the house and she was just on the telephone, then we quickly retreated before she saw us.

Most of the time though, Mrs. Corelle just put us to work. The girls were responsible for the endless pile of laundry in a house full of kids. They would sometimes stay up all night doing the laundry for the entire household of thirteen people. The piles of laundry were deep and completely covered the floor in the rather large laundry room. I, a five-year-old, would do the dishes every night for thirteen people. I could not go to bed until I had finished them.

These were just a small part of the long list of chores we did.

We learned very quickly that if we did not do our chores completely and at the speed that had been requested we would get our hair pulled, our face slapped or punched, or have our heads slammed together as punishment.

Our job was to stay out of Mrs. Corelle's way and do our chores, nothing else. All of us kids saw some pretty late nights, which were almost every night. If we finished one chore, then we were immediately given another. We were merely tolerated for the paycheck the Corelles got from the State for fostering us. We served no other purpose. And she let us know she could not stand the sight of us.

Any time she would walk into the room, we would scurry away and hide. She would leave the home often but that did not make things better at all because we were left under the watch of the older sons of the Corelles and some of their cousins who stayed there sometimes. They would beat and molest us daily while Mrs. Corelle would be out of the house for hours.

These teens wouldn't call Nina by her name. They only called her Dog.

Sometimes they would put a pillow over my face so I couldn't breathe. When they took the pillow off, I would gasp for air and beg for water. Then they would spit in my mouth.

Several times, the older boys rolled me up in an area rug where I couldn't move or breathe. They left me like that for hours.

We were in this home for almost two years.

The Corelles were very involved in the Catholic Church and we never missed a Sunday service. Mrs. Corelle would put on her huge golden-brown wig and polish up her now enormous family and parade us around that church like she was so proud of all the good she was doing in the world, especially for these poor, helpless five children. The entire church perceived her as a very good woman. Little did anyone in that congregation know that we would be returning to a living hell the moment after she shook the priest's hand and we had piled into the van to return home.

Ronald

Ronald seemed to have latched onto me and took me under his wing for the first week or so that we were in that home. He would help me tie my shoes for church, and he gave me a rosary. We went to church, but it seemed weird to me. The only other church I had been to in the past was a Baptist Church. This was the first time I saw nuns. Ronald was an altar boy and became my friend, or at least so I thought.

One evening, I saw Ronald go into my bedroom instead of his. I thought he might be going in to steal my toys, but when I entered Ronald was waiting alone for me on his knees. I sensed that something was wrong and tried to go back down the stairs. He pulled me back and pulled my pants down. He was bigger and overpowering. I tried to pull away, but I had to mind him as he was much older and bigger than me and he was my buddy—after all, he had helped me tie my shoes. From then on, he molested me in many ways every day. No amount of avoiding him or fighting him off could stop him.

Any day that Ronald planned on sneaking into my room in the night he would tell me not to wear underwear. I would try to avoid him after dinner. But he would find me and tell me to hide in the bathroom and wait. There he would take his clothes off and lay on top of me. I felt I had to do what he said. I was five. And he was big.

When I began to resist him too much, he told me that he would go do it to my sisters and brothers instead, so I would stop fighting. I later found out that he was going to their rooms anyway. In time, another Corelle son, Lyle, started molesting us as well.

Mrs. Corelle caught Ronald doing it once in the middle of the night and surprisingly called DHS. They came to the house in the middle of the night. They made Ronald promise not to do it again and sent us back to bed. The next day, a therapist from DHS came to the house and sat us all down together. They were told that Lyle, one of the older boys, had also been molesting me and the others. They made our two older foster brothers promise that they wouldn't do it again and then they made myself and my sisters promise that we would tell them if the boys tried. This was the extent of the punishment.

Obviously, the only ones satisfied with the conversation were the DHS social workers because the abuse never stopped.

The Corelles were very bad people that were sick, delusional, selfish, and extremely cruel. They allowed a lot of bad things to happen while they were in charge.

We were only an income to them. Every head of every boy and girl in the house was just a paycheck. Usually, I can find redeeming qualities even in the worst of people. There were none to be found in this family. They were all very bad people, not just people who did bad things.

Spokane, Washington

The Corelles took us with their kids, Ronald, Lyle, Karen, Sal, and Joel to Spokane, Washington. They moved us there and social services never checked on us to discover that we were gone, even after many neighbors had turned the family in because they could hear our screaming during our beatings all the way from their houses. The Corelles rented an RV and a U-Haul and we took a three-month trip and stayed in RV parks on the way there. We saw Mount Rushmore, the Petrified Forest, and a few other landmarks along the route.

Sue was eight and I was five. These were great sites to see that we entirely appreciated as young kids. We also did get to do a lot of fun things in the RV parks and elsewhere during the trip, but then we had to come back to the camper and deal with the reality of this family.

We were in Spokane for a year and then Mrs. Corelle told us they were being made to come back to Arkansas. What she didn't tell us was that the Social Services Department in Arkansas had finally realized something very bad was going on because reports had been made eighteen different times by neighbors and friends who were concerned about our safety, and Arkansas DHS needed us to be closer to them so they could watch over us easier. The DHS office must've been pretty persistent because we drove straight through the day and night and arrived about twenty-four hours later in North Little Rock, Arkansas.

The Arkansas DHS workers started to periodically come to the house and would separately and privately ask me and my siblings a bunch of questions about how things were going. Then they would have a private conversation with the Corelles as well, while us kids nervously waited in another room, hoping we would not get beat up when the DHS workers left because we had said something wrong.

Mrs. Corelle had a calculated way of making sure we didn't talk. The agency would plan the visits. So, just before they came, she took us shopping or bought us ice cream or did other nice things. She told us how much she loved us and bribed us. Mixing that approach with some heavy threats seemed always to produce a good review from DHS. Even so, the social workers maintained their doubts.

A Saint She Ain't

Mrs. Corelle got a big paycheck for housing a handicapped child. I remember us kids sitting around the living room watching a *Jerry's Kids Telethon* on TV when Mrs. Corelle entered, pushing the young, adopted girl, Karen, in a wheelchair. Everybody in the community thought she was saving this kid and saving the world. And she liked the exposure. But the truth was we were all scared for our lives around her, including the two-year-old crippled girl in the wheelchair.

Mrs. Corelle had a violent and explosive temper and would beat us daily. I remember how I made the mistake of standing next to her once, watching her cook while she was on the phone. Apparently I was not welcome there because she turned and hit me in the face with the edge of the frying pan in which she was cooking a grilled cheese sandwich. The sandwich went flying across the room and the pan burned my eyebrow and cut my face deeply. My eyebrow was flipped inside out from the gaping wound on my face. She handed me a washcloth wrapped over ice, then resumed her phone call.

To this day, I still have a scar that reminds me of that moment. I see it every time I look into a mirror. I never was taken to the doctor and I stayed home from school until the gash healed along with the black eye that accompanied the deep cut.

I would spend a lot of time thinking about excuses to tell people who asked me about all of the bruises and marks on my body from my foster mother's beatings. A lot of times she would send us to school with a ready excuse that she had given us. And the excuses for the bruises always worked. Everyone wants to think that the reason a child is so beat up is because they play hard and not because he is being mercilessly beaten on a daily basis at home.

One glorious day, I went to school with the whole left side of my face bruised and my eye swollen shut. I had an obvious handprint on my face. Though I told my teacher and the principal I had fallen down the stairs, they could see it was undeniably a handprint. For a while they had had their suspicions of the Corelles like everyone else. Finally, they had proof.

Mrs. Corelle had been trying to teach me how to brush my teeth and she kept slapping my face as I tried to do her bidding. I remember sitting on the sink and being unsure of what she wanted me to do. She just kept knocking the holy hell right out of me. Every repeating smack would whip my head around and I would see my face in the mirror for an instant—each time seeing the progression of swelling and redness getting worse, and not understanding why this beating was happening. She'd hand me the toothbrush and say, "Now do it again," and I'd do it again and then she would hit me and leave another handprint. Apparently, I wasn't supposed to swallow the toothpaste, but I didn't quite understand that this was what the problem was.

The next day, armed with the excuse that I had fallen down the stairs, I went to school as usual. I was sitting at my desk and writing the numbers 1 to 100 on my Big Chief writing tablet with an illustration of a Native American man in a feathered headdress on the cover, as we did every morning in kindergarten before the bell rang to begin our school day. I was doing this when my teacher walked up to me, grabbed my face, and gasped loudly. It scared me instantly because I was aware that she understood the full implications of my bruises. My first thought was that I was in trouble.

The teacher quickly walked out of the room and was gone for a long time. When she reappeared, she came with the principal and they asked me to follow them to his office. On the way there, I remember thinking I was in a lot of trouble and felt my scalp and ears burning with shame. My teacher was holding my hand so tightly and walking so fast that I thought she was angry at me. Looking back on it now, I understand that she was just in a mad panic to save this child. Apparently she had reported the Corelles several times before and this was finally going to verify her suspicions.

My two sisters were already in the principal's office with policemen when we arrived. Sue must've seen how extremely frightened I was because she grabbed my hand the moment I walked in and never let it go. We were all afraid because we knew that if they didn't believe us then we would have to go back to the Corelle house where we would receive another severe beating for telling on them.

It seemed to us like adults always found a way to excuse Mrs. Corelle. But this time was different. I could feel it.

On April 1, 1983, it was decided that we should be removed. The police escorted us back to the home where we quickly put all of our belongings into black trash bags, one bag for each kid. We did this very fast because we were afraid the adults would change their minds. We were then put together in the back of a police car. I remember standing up in the back seat of the car and facing backwards to watch the house disappear behind us in the distance and knowing that we were finally free.

Mrs. Corelle stood staring out of the window with a somber look on her face. I imagine she was contemplating where her next paycheck was going to come from.

Splitting Us Up

The Gateleys had moved on from the shelter but would come back and visit us periodically. They had since moved to Westfork, Arkansas, a tiny town three hours north in the mountains. When they saw we were going in and out of foster homes again and being beaten in each situation, they finally told the DHS, "Bring them to us." We were as special to them as they were to us.

The Gateleys turned their house into a therapeutic foster home to try to help us and to save us from more abuse. It was the whole reason they did it! They got a license so they could take all of us in and we could stop being bounced around between horrible places.

That would be our last stop before the DHS began finding us individual foster homes one by one. We would all end up getting adopted by different families.

They took photos of us individually to put in our files and to send to our potential new families. When my siblings' pictures were taken, the left side of my face was still bruised from Mrs. Corelle's last beating and I was told I couldn't have my photo taken until the bruising was gone. Because I knew that I didn't have a chance of a new family until I could get my picture made, I asked every single day if my face was ready to have my picture made to send to my new family.

We stayed at the Gateley's new foster home for six months while they found us each a family. We would wait our turns and then get picked up to go meet a potential family. Eventually, after a few visits, we would end up spending the night or a long weekend to see if it was a good match.

CHAPTER SEVEN

Failure of the System

"You may choose to look the other way, but you can never say again that you did not know."

—WILLIAM WILBERFORCE

We lived in many foster homes. Due to the severity of the abuse that we endured, our 1983 court case led several foster care and adoption laws to be changed, and to child welfare-safeguarding procedures being put in place, including mandatory surprise visits, background checks, financial checks, and mandatory classes on parenting. Foster parents would now be required to take these classes, a whole six-week curriculum. One subject lesson in the curriculum was specifically for situations that foster parents might get into and how they would handle them.

Kadushin's list of abuse, which is part of a framework in the child welfare field, is used by social workers as a guideline to assess situations such as our family faced. It defines what constitutes abuse. When we were finally taken out of the Corelle home, we had experienced every single abuse on that list. In fact, they had to add three more types of abuse to the list based on our experiences.

One of the laws that was changed was the limit to how many kids can be put in a home at the same time. This way, the DHS system can't just keep adding more kids to one household.

Before this, the more kids foster parents could take into their homes, the more checks they received and there was no limit. So, greedy people just kept piling more and more children into their homes and raking in the money with little care given to any actual child.

Another law that was changed was that before our case they could just throw kids in there and not come back and get them, or even check on them periodically. Our case ensures that foster parents now have to allow surprise visits.

These changes are a very good result that came from a very bad situation!

How the System Failed Us

Some examples of abuse can be found in the family intake report that I uncovered at a guidance center we went to in Arkansas while living with the Corelles. In this report, it says:

- Mr. Corelle spanks the children too harshly.

- The children are given too much responsibility at home.
- Sexual abuse by Ronald and Lyle to the Dennis boy and girls has been reported and is confirmed. (So, they knew it, yet we were left in the home.)
- Mrs. Corelle admits she often leaves the children in the care of her sons Ronald, who is mentally retarded, and Lyle, who is an alcoholic.

Instead of removing us from that house, the DHS report states that they "got a commitment from the girls and Patrick [me, Cody] that if anything happens again they will tell their [foster] mom. We feel comfortable the children will do this." Apparently these personnel were the only ones feeling comfortable, because we certainly were not. The abuse did not stop until the school called the police.

The report also confirmed that Mr. Corelle was the only one who finally admitted whipping us for lying and not doing our chores. (A lie he told.) "No attempt was made to remove the children as they did not appear to be in imminent danger." (A failure of the person writing the report to protect us.)

Despite all of that evidence of abuse, we were not removed from that house until the day the teacher saw the handprint on my face at the school!

How Many Drugs Can We Give This Kid?

When I was a kid, I was put on Ritalin. I was diagnosed with attention deficit hyperactivity disorder (ADHD), obsessive-compulsive disorder (OCD), and possible Tourette syndrome. At that time, I was the only kid in my whole entire school that took Ritalin. The drug was meant to calm me down. This was back before many people were diagnosed with these disorders.

I was given special permission to walk alone to the school nurse at lunch to get my pill. I felt like it was a privilege to do this. When they realized that I still had tons of energy and a lack of focus even on this medication, they brought in a refrigerator box and cut out one side. They put my desk in the back of the classroom for two years and stood this refrigerator box around me. Being the fantastic artist I was, I just pretty much covered the inside of that refrigerator box with drawings of horses. Nobody was slowing me down!

These days, I believe it's obvious to everybody in child education that this sort of stigmatic isolation is the worst thing you could do for a child with attention deficit and zero self-esteem.

Seven years later, when I was living in the Children's Home at the age of fifteen, I received mandatory counseling once a week. The school bus would drop me off at a psychiatric clinic on the way home. There they would ask me all kinds of questions, like had I checked my doorknob twice to make sure it was locked? Or had I checked my alarm settings twice? Things like that. I would say yes, and the doctor would quickly say, "Okay, here's a prescription. You have OCD."

For my part, I thought, *Shouldn't I double-check my alarm?* I was just being thorough.

Each time I would go see the counselor they would pile on more medications for more things that seemed made up. It felt like they were using me and the other kids at the center as guinea pigs to test new medications that had just come out. Basically, all of the kids at the children's home were on some kind of medication and most were taking several kinds. Every morning and evening there would be a long line of kids waiting to be handed their medications, and we were watched closely to be sure we swallowed them.

Those medications did not seem to fix any problem but only to cause more. I had several emotional breakdowns because I did not want to take the medication or because the medication was wrong for me and not working. Several kids that I kept in contact with from the children's home ended up having drug addictions in their adult lives.

When I left the children's home two and a half years later, the administrators told me to be sure to keep taking the medications. Internally, I was like, *No, thank you.* I had a big self-realization at the age of seventeen that all the things everyone had told me about myself that they thought were negative or needed to be changed were really some of the best things about me.

They had me on seven different medications, all of which were deconstructing me. All of the things I loved about myself, those medications were taking away. Because I was becoming a monotone version of myself, I took myself off all the medications and learned how to embrace who I am and who I am meant to be. My ADHD, including hyperactivity and feeling my full range of emotions to their maximum extent, ended up just meaning that I can't focus on one thing, but I can focus on ten things at once. As an adult, I've become a master of multitasking. Along with my overactive mind, these qualities grew to be some of my greatest strengths in life.

To be clear, I don't believe that people who actually need these medications should stop taking them. And in fact, I feel like stopping taking medication abruptly or without professional support can be a huge problem. So many times, people who need the medications and take them begin to balance out and start feeling like they don't need the medicine anymore, because it's working. Then they stop and all their problems come flooding back and the cycle begins again.

This was not the case in my situation. They were giving me medication for depression, but I was sitting in a children's home with no family and far away from anyone I knew and loved. Of course, I was going to feel sad and lonely. Medication was not the right answer.

Sue: A Cinderella Story

My sister Sue went through a couple of foster homes. One home had the intention of adopting her but soon sent her back because the parents decided they wanted a boy instead of a girl. Another time, foster parents drove from three hours away to pick her up. They barely spoke to her on the long drive back to her new home, finally arriving around midnight. The couple led her from the garage into the kitchen with her suitcase still in hand. They all paused there and looked around the kitchen. The counters were covered in large piles of moldy pots, pans, and dishes with old food caked on them. Their dining room looked the same, like they had not done dishes in years, but had just kept piling them on any surface they could find.

Right after they walked in the house, these people said, "As soon as all those dishes are done, there's a couch down in the basement for you to sleep on."

These were two teachers with three teenage daughters of their own. You would think that someone in the household could have done this cleaning at any time. Chores like this was something we were all too familiar with, but Sue had thought we had left this form of abuse back at the Corelles. She managed to get all of the dishes done, went down to the basement and slept on the raggedy old couch. The next day they told her they were going to convert their office room into her bedroom. She spent the next two weeks packing up all their books and moving all their office stuff out of this bedroom. She didn't mind this so much, as she was preparing her own room and making a space for herself. Although it would have been nice if they had this prepared for her in some sort of welcoming attempt before she got there.

She finally finished and was completely satisfied with her new room, but still not quite sure what to make of this new situation. But as soon as she had it all done and ready to move into, the oldest of the family's three natural daughters decided it looked really nice and took the room for herself. So, Sue was sent back down to the basement.

Their daughters found out (probably from their parents) about the history of sexual abuse that was done to Sue in the past. The daughters went back to the school, told all the kids at her new middle school what happened to her and how our mother had "sold her into prostitution." A solid twist on the actual story, but not wrong really. It became very hard for her to be at the school after that as she was being called a whore and a prostitute.

And the girls also constantly beat her up.

When Christmas came around, Sue wasn't allowed to go to the Christmas gathering with them at their grandparents' house because she wasn't a real "family member." The grandparents' house was just across the field from their own. Sue spent that Christmas sitting on the front porch all by herself watching that house from across the field and imagining all the Christmas cheer that must have been going on inside.

The family came home that afternoon and she was allowed to go with them to another family member's house; and since they weren't expecting her for Christmas that year, she was handed five yards of corduroy material as her Christmas gift. I guess they thought she could make something out of it. Sue had learned a lot of grownup skills in our few short years, but sewing her own clothes was not one of them. (She was only twelve years old.)

Two weeks later, after Christmas was her birthday. She was so excited, as she thought she would get a card or presents or something, or maybe even hear from her siblings. We did not really know where she was, however. I knew she lived a few hours from me at this point, but every time I attempted to contact her I couldn't get anyone to answer or return my messages.

The whole day went by, nothing happened. And the next day nothing happened. A week later she got a "Sorry I forgot your birthday" card from one of the foster parents and that was it.

She was never allowed to participate in any of the family events. She had to always be home by herself or was left alone with the three foster sisters who would gang up and beat on her the whole time. She was a really tough little girl at this point but there were three of them. It was extremely obvious that she was just brought there to clean the house and do whatever the three girls didn't want to do. It was basically a Cinderella story but without the prince to rescue her.

In the end, she rescued herself.

A counselor would come by once a week who would take her from school to KFC to eat, always on a Wednesday. They had a meeting after she had been with this horrible family for about six to eight months at which she told him again how tired of it all she was and how she just couldn't take it anymore. That counselor told her the most important thing she ever heard in her life that day at KFC. "You are the only one responsible for your happiness." When he took her back to school, those magic words kept ringing in her ears. Sue went straight to the foster mother who happened to be the reading teacher at the school. She swung open the door to the woman's classroom and without any hesitation spewed these beautiful words. "You are a fucking bitch, and I will not be your fucking slave anymore."

Our childhood with our mother taught us some colorful and sometimes very useful words. Sue shut the door as swiftly as she had opened it and went directly to the principal's office and picked up the phone, called 911 and told them what highway the DHS could find her on, where exactly she was heading, and that her days with this family were over.

She knew exactly where to get help.

After Sue hung up the phone, she walked right out the door and onto the highway. Walking the highway was extremely familiar to us as well. Since she had told the 911 operator her specific plans and where she would be, it wasn't long until a car with two social workers in it pulled up next to her while she was stomping her way down the highway.

Sue had reached her limit with being bounced around foster homes while her four siblings had already been in their permanent homes for a long time at this point. She decided to take matters into her own hands. Without hesitation, she hopped right in the car and told those social workers the new plan. The only way she was ever going to be adopted was if she went with a certain family and that family only! That family was the Gateleys, the very first family we had met the day we'd gone to the shelter when we were separated from our mother, and the only people other than our brothers and sisters, who had ever truly been there for her.

The social workers contacted the Gateleys who agreed for her to be placed there temporarily until they could figure out another plan. Two years later, she was still living with the Gateleys, so naturally they adopted her. I don't think Sue or the Gateleys ever truly thought this was a temporary thing. Sue had finally found her forever mom and dad.

CHAPTER EIGHT

Becoming Jonathan Cody Renegar

"To be yourself in a world that is constantly trying to make you something else is the greatest accomplishment."
—RALPH WALDO EMERSON

Meeting the Renegars and Seeing the House

The Gateleys were assisting DHS to set up my individual adoption and my siblings'. As part of this process, it was arranged that I would meet with the Renegars at a fast-food restaurant. I didn't understand who these people were or why I was being sent off to have lunch with them. For a while it was extremely awkward and then it dawned on me what this occasion was all about. Halfway through the meal, I asked if they were going to be my new family. I noticed awkward glances they gave each other just before the dad of the family replied, "We're going to see about that."

A few weeks after that lunch, Mr. and Mrs. Renegar came to pick me up at the foster home where I was living with the Gateleys in West Fork, Arkansas, and took me out to their house. As we drove down the road, I tried to guess which house was ours. *Is that our house? Or that one?* The biggest, most beautiful house was across a large, green field. I hadn't even considered that one when they pointed at it and said, "That's our house." Arabian horses were running beside the car as we drove up to it on the long driveway. Mr. Renegar owned a timber mill in the town of Happy Valley, where he was prominent in the business community.

Once we parked and stepped out of the car, a little white dog ran up to me. I stood there holding that little dog and looked around as I always did on arrival at a new placement to size it up. Perched between two giant oak trees, I saw a cool-looking tree house and a tire swing. And in a side yard between the house and a barn, there was a chicken coop. In a separate field from where the horses were, there were tons of brown cows! The whole thing was dreamy. It was the most beautiful place I'd ever seen! I thought I was finally safe. This was the safe haven I had always longed for. I just wished my sisters and brothers could share it with me.

A Pact

My siblings and I desperately missed each other and were very concerned about how each of us was adjusting in our new home. Of course, we wanted to stay in touch. My new family also seemed like they wanted us to do so. But then, on my eighth birthday, when all of my brothers and sisters came over for a pool party and we managed to sneak off for some private time, just us kids, I learned I was mistaken.

We were sitting on the trampoline, talking together about everything that had happened in the past few months when Nina said that her new parents had told her this would be our last visit. She said that all of the sets of new parents had agreed that they didn't want us to see each other anymore because they were afraid we wouldn't bond with them if we did.

I could certainly see from their standpoint how our wanting to keep to ourselves might seem troublesome, but in this situation, given we had just survived hell, were they really saying they were not even going to let us talk to each other?! We had been promised so many times that we would be able to keep in touch. We felt completely betrayed and lied to by Nina's news.

Right then and there, we made a pact. Of course, my two older sisters, as usual, had already worked this out in their heads. We would all "act up" and raise hell with our new families so we could get sent back. We instructed my younger brothers how to do everything—

how to kick, bite, scream, and be as horrible as they could to "make them not want you." This way, in our minds, they would all have to send us away and we would be together again, forever.

Well, the parents found out about our pact. I don't know who squealed on us, but eventually all of the new parents caved and agreed they would allow us to see each other a couple of times a year. Sometimes this would be on one of our birthdays or it would be at Christmas—times like that. Because of this accession to our desire to stay connected, we agreed to comply and act normal.

Ultimately, those visits ended up occurring only about once a year. When we got older, we would sneak around, hide in different rooms or closets, or wait until the parents in our homes were gone and then call each other. They were not going to keep us apart, ever!

The Grass Is Not Greener

The gleam of my shiny new home faded quickly as it became exceedingly obvious that the Renegars had adopted me to please themselves and not for me. The Renegars had three daughters. Mr. Renegar's brother had three girls as well. Therefore, they had no boys in the family to carry on the Renegar name. This was the reason they wanted me to come live with them. My sole purpose was to be that necessary boy.

Before I went to live with them, they had sent me several letters that described the man they wanted me to grow up to be. They were very specific. What the letters told me was how they wanted me to play guitar for their church when I was old enough and to become a hunter. And they described how I would grow into a mighty Christian man under their guidance.

I had been to churches many times before but never really understood why I was there. I was just now becoming old enough to grasp the idea of religion, but still had no interest in it.

When you adopt a seven-year-old child, you're not adopting a blank slate. It is not possible to erase the things that have happened to this child. Don't expect the seven-year-old who has had more pain in his short years on the earth than most people endure in a lifetime will be your polished-up little show pony to parade around your church and show everybody what a good deed you've done.

I needed help. I did not need to be a show pony, I just needed unconditional love. This was not the home for that. I needed a somewhat safe environment, counseling, and time to heal. I already missed my brothers and sisters, as any child in my situation would. And I was holding out hope that it would get easier and that my tears at night would soon fade away.

Unfortunately, the Renegars were never interested in who I was, only the boy they could turn me into. The only aspect of my personality that they seemed to approve of and validate was my artistic streak. They liked the fact I knew how to draw (though they might not like the picture I am drawing of them here). I think my ability to draw was the one thing they could spin to make this trashy little boy look like maybe he was just a little eccentric but still classy.

The Renegars desperately wanted a son but with every attempt they made themselves would have another girl. They had the name Jonathan picked out for this son who never came. When they eventually adopted me, in court, they changed my first name from Patrick to Jonathan. I kept my middle name, Cody.

After knowing them well for many years, I can imagine the very specific type of person they had envisioned their son being when they thought of him. They must have pictured Jonathan as a God-fearing leading actor sort of kid, the kind of kid who carried the mantle of the Renegar name as if it was some sort of grandiose dynasty. He would be the perfect collective reflection of his parents. A straight A student. Charming and extremely easy to love. Beloved by all.

Jonathan's parents probably visualized talking with their friends about their perfect son. People would not see this as an empty kind of bragging but would admire their tremendous pride in what they had created in this boy. They would take him to every football game and church event. It would be that kind of pride that would cause them to buy him his first car. He would have two different and equally wonderful, happy relationships with his parents. His mother's friends might giggle about how he was going to be such a lady's man. She would smile and ignore this, instead talking about his interest in studying law after college at a university with a big name. Just like in the movies.

This was the picture-perfect future that they had in mind for me, but much to the Renegars' dismay they quickly learned I was not going to be that kind of boy. I spent many years trying to become this Jonathan. I wanted badly to please them, even though only weeks after they adopted me they revealed I was not anything like the boy they had dreamed of having for so long. I was a good boy. I did what I was told. I was kind, loving, and respectful. They managed to dilute my very strong southern accent into something a little more polished. They taught me to stand up straight, to enunciate my words, and to speak strong and proper. Still, I was Cody. I was not, and never would be, Jonathan.

There was no room for flaws in the Jonathan they had expected.

Living with the Renegars

In the Renegar household, I wasn't permitted to watch my two favorite shows, *I Dream of Jeanie* or *Bewitched*, because the Renegars were religious. They believed those shows had sorcery in them and sorcery was from Satan. When they weren't around, I would always sneak and watch the shows. When I turned eighteen, I bought an entire DVD set of both those shows.

When they first adopted me, the superhero He-Man (played in the sci-fi movie *Masters of the Universe* by the Swedish actor Dolph Lundgren) was very popular. I was really into the line of toys and the animated TV show. A couple months later, for my first Christmas with them, the presents under the tree completed my entire He-Man collection. A few months later, they went on a religious mission trip to Honduras for two weeks. When they came back, they quickly burned all my He-Man action figures because they said *He-Man* contained satanic symbolism. They replaced these with a collection of G.I. Joe action figures. I had never heard of G.I. Joe at this point, but I quickly learned to love it.

Meanwhile, if they had only known that I used to take my sisters' Barbies and dress them in leaves to pretend they were elf people living in the trees, their heads might have exploded. Or I might have been ambushed and taken somewhere secret for an exorcism.

One day, when I was about seven years old, my new parents sat me down—this was just a few weeks after I had moved in. We sat together at the kitchen table and they said, "We want to introduce you to our friend Jesus." The way they said it, I thought some really cool guy was going to come over for dinner. But no.

They started to explain to me about Adam and Eve. They brought out a children's picture book and read from it as they aimed the illustrations in my direction. I didn't understand what this had to do with their friend who was coming to visit. Once I finally realized that they were trying to tell me about their beliefs and their friend Jesus, I could tell they were very serious, they weren't playing around. I knew I didn't believe what they were saying, but I let them finish. At the end of their presentation, they asked, "What do you think of all of that?"

I looked at my adoptive mom and said, "I don't believe that." Although I had heard similar stories in the Sunday schools I had attended and in the pews of various churches we had been bounced through when I was younger, I was just old enough to get a little bit more of a grasp now on what they were talking about. And I knew I didn't believe it. Frankly, I also couldn't believe that they believed it. At first, I thought they were trying to play a trick on me or that this was a joke of some sort. Their expressions and demeanor immediately changed when they heard my answer. Though I guessed it would displease them, I courageously stood my ground and told them I did not believe what they were telling me. Their excitement faded after that, and they looked at me a little differently from then on.

My adoptive mom stood up from the table and abruptly walked off. My adoptive dad started to try to explain what he'd already said in more depth because he thought maybe I just didn't understand it and it just needed to be repeated. Then after a few minutes of my adoptive mom thinking and brewing in the other room, she emerged with an announcement. "God told me that there's a demon that has a hold of you."

I was like, "Wait, what? Now there's demons?" I was only seven, but I was old enough to think that these people were crazy.

From that moment on, she never warmed up to me again. She acted extremely cold toward me for the next eight years. All hope was lost that I would ever again have a mother.

Play Guitar for Jesus or Don't Play Guitar at All

One time, I asked my adoptive parents to take me so I could buy a small guitar that I had my eyes on for a long time. Even though learning to play guitar was a part of their grand plan for me, I personally pictured myself sitting around a cowboy campfire with a horse and playing tunes to the stars on it. I had been saving my allowance from the Gateleys' home and now from this new home for many months.

I wanted that guitar more than I can tell you! I thought about it constantly. Every day I would get out my money and count it to see how close I was to the $40 it would take to buy the guitar. Any time we went to Walmart I would make it a point to stop by that guitar on the shelf and give it a good stare, for as long as I was allowed. I would even take it down and try to play the strings through the plastic packaging.

Now I had finally saved enough money by doing extra chores and along with my allowance that I was ready to buy the guitar.

In response to my request, my parents told me that they would let me get the guitar on one condition, which was that I would play it in their church.

This wasn't a negotiation I was willing to participate in. I did not understand the church or the strange pressure I was getting to participate in their beliefs. Because I didn't understand it, I was naturally pushing back anytime it was mentioned.

I decided not to buy that guitar after all.

CHAPTER NINE

And So, It Began Again

"We don't owe you anything, just food and a roof over your head. Everything else is extra."
—MY ADOPTIVE PARENTS

The Newness Wears Off

Once, I was working in the yard with my newly adoptive father and I did something that caused him to snap at me. Due to my past experiences, I was very scared of men, so any little thing like this could cause me to go into survival mode. I could either hide or run. Those were the only two tools I had. I hadn't been there long and didn't know how he operated, so when he got upset, my instinctive reaction was to take off running to avoid the inevitable hurt that would come from an adult in a bad temper. I was fast and could dodge in and out of any obstacle. That was how I had learned to survive and, after years of practice, I had become very quick about my escapes.

When he spoke to me sternly, I started running and he started chasing. I ran around trees, under fences, and leaped over hay bales. The chase came down to us both just running circles around the wheelbarrow. I stopped when I managed to get the wheelbarrow between us, using it as a barrier. I obviously hadn't thought this through, however, because his arm was long enough to simply reach over the wheelbarrow. He grabbed me by my hair and lifted me up to suspend me in the air inches from his face as he began scolding me with an angry tone which I had only ever heard from my mother and Mrs. Corelle, who were both violent people.

This time, the threat was coming from a large man who had promised to protect me. The only dad I'd ever known.

As I hung there trying to ease my pain by holding onto his arm with both hands and looking right into his eyes, he spoke low, slow, and deep as little bits of spit flew from his mouth and landed on my face. "Don't you ever run from me again, boy."

I am certain that this situation would have frustrated any parent on the planet. But this man knew the kid he had adopted: a fragile child who had just been separated from his four siblings and who had been beaten and molested and starved and would likely be emotionally disturbed for his whole life. The rules of patience seem to dictate that he should have gone a little further to be tolerant of me in this situation—

especially since I had only known them for merely a few short months.

When Mr. Renegar was finished making his threats and laying down the new law, he let go of my hair and effortlessly flung me onto the grass. I stood up as fast as I could with my heels slipping in the grass behind me, and this time I ran straight into the house and sat on the staircase just off of the living room. I was sobbing alone with my arms crossed and my head laid on my knees when my adoptive mother walked by and asked me what was wrong. I hoped that she would come to my rescue. She was absolutely the only one that could have saved me. What she did then would set the tone for the rest of my life with them. The moment could go either way.

I looked up at her through my streaming tears and explained what had just transpired in the front yard. I was desperately hoping she would sit next to me and hold me, or race to the yard to scold my new father for being mean. I wanted her to protect me so he could never ever hurt me. But when I looked up, I was met with an expressionless, icy stare that seemed to still be processing. After a few moments she replied with, "Well, the newness wears off of you pretty quickly." She then turned and walked off, leaving me with the distinct, heavy realization that I would never be safe anywhere.

These people had been my last hope. Now hope was gone. That small phrase that she said to me in my moment of helplessness has haunted me all of my life.

When someone says they're trying to heal from their childhood, it's things like this that stand out the most.

Maybe they don't know it when they say it, but one small phrase said at the wrong time can poison someone's mind until the day they die. We have to actively seek out these tainted ideas in our own minds and dismantle them, because they are poison and we ourselves are the only ones with the antidote.

From then on, I was constantly performing for the Renegars, trying to be as charming, cheerful, happy, bright, and as colorful as I possibly could so that the newness never wore off of me. I subsequently took this into my relationships as an adult. My romantic relationships, my family relationships, and my friendships. Always waiting for the novelty of Cody to fade away, I was constantly worried that the proverbial other shoe would drop, and someone would see the real me underneath the huge performance I was putting on. They'd see that I was just a broken little boy still trying to stand as tall as he possibly could in hopes that love would find him someday.

I've since learned that the truest, most beautiful form of love comes when you allow someone to see your weakest parts. Not by constantly carrying around a victim state of mind or whining about the wrongdoings that happened to you. But by not hiding when you're sad, mad, happy, or whatever. Don't hide, let your feelings show because this will attract people to you who will love you for who you are. Let them see you in all of your spectacular glory and in all of your horrible darkness on your saddest days. Be yourself with those glorious emotions, as big as you possibly can be, and true love will find you right there!

If you are trying to be someone else or hide any part of you, then whatever love you attract won't be true. So, just be your genuine self and save yourself a lot of heartache.

No Harm Was Meant, Yet Much Harm Was Done

My adoptive dad looked and acted like a young Mel Gibson. He was extremely fit, very charming, and the hardest working man I've ever known. He wanted to be a good father. He seemed to me to be a great father to his three biological daughters, although, in retrospect, I do remember him calling the oldest one stupid and kicking her so hard in her butt once that he broke her tailbone. He also called her stupid a lot.

Years later, she found out she was dyslexic. I hope he felt like shit after hearing of that diagnosis. Or at least that he apologized profusely and made it up to her somehow.

The three girls were all extremely beautiful. The oldest and youngest ones seemed put off that I was adopted and constantly annoyed that I even existed. Usually, the only time they didn't ignore me was to tell me to get out of their way. But even so, the middle daughter, Penelope, constantly defended me when my adoptive dad was being cruel to me. She did this quite often. I believe she thought that the cruel times she witnessed were the only cruel experiences I had. But in reality, I was alone in the house with two adults who completely despised me. I was nothing like the Jonathan they had dreamed of and I finally stopped "performing" for them and became hell-bent on just being who I was and no one else. All three of the girls were much older than me and left for college soon after I was adopted.

It would make sense that my adoptive dad picked up his scary disciplinary tactics from his own father, who was a very stern man who had been a lieutenant colonel in the military. Apparently, he had also used very harsh and violent corporal punishment on his two sons. This is the man my adoptive father learned discipline from, and he did not break the cycle of violence. I think he knew deep down he was doing something wrong. And I even believe he meant well. He believed he was beating demons out of me. No harm was meant, but much harm was done.

He beat me many times and sometimes he would have me spank him instead, because he said he was taking my punishment, like Jesus took our punishment on the cross. Becoming the martyr or sacrificing himself. Sometimes my father would just pretend he was spanking me to appease my mom who wanted me properly punished. If he didn't feel I deserved a punishment, he'd bend his belt in half and pop it against itself to make it sound like he was hitting me. I'd do a fake scream so she would hear it from the other room and think I had been whipped.

That alone shows me that he knew he was going way too far.

If someone is trying to hide what they are doing from someone else in this way, then that person knows what he is doing is wrong.

Many of the harshest sessions of punishment would take place in the barn. He would take me to the saddle room, tie my hands over a saddle with my shirt over my head and my pants to my ankles, and whip me relentlessly. All the while I was taking the beating, he would demand for me to accept God into my heart and admit that who I was was wrong.

I could've saved myself years of physical torture by just admitting this and playing the part, but I just couldn't find it in my soul to do that.

Internally, I struggled to understand everything about Christianity in the Bible that I possibly could. I was in a Christian school where we had Bible classes and I had access to all of the biblical knowledge I could stomach. I would search and study relentlessly. It actually became a slight obsession of mine to understand this religion because I thought that maybe once I had truly understood it and believed it I could finally stand up one day and tell this man that I did. I hoped he would hug me and love me and accept me and stop hurting me then. But that day would never come.

My adoptive mom would punish me by just giving me bread and water as a meal just before sending me to bed. She considered herself a fantastic cook so she felt that's how she would make me suffer.

There were, of course, normal days in between the dark ones but they never quite worked out well and in almost every experience we had together my adoptive dad would always be yelling at me, hitting or slapping me, or just being disapproving. Almost daily, he told me that I was not going to amount to anything. Even when we would do typical father-son things together, these would always be ruined by his violent temper and end with me crying and bruised or bleeding.

Like when he was teaching me how to drive. He repeatedly punched me in the shoulder because I kept popping the clutch too quickly. By the end of my lesson, I couldn't even lift my right arm anymore to move the gear shift. When he punched me the last time, I got out of the car and walked home.

I remember that day very well because I fully expected to turn around and see him chasing me down to beat me or kick me into the ditch on the side of the road. But he didn't. When we finally met up back at home, he acted like nothing had happened. So, that tells me that he knew he had lost his temper and he must have felt some remorse.

My adoptive dad apologized to me many times after he had administered a violent beating or lost his temper and said horrible things to me that no child should hear from his father. That did show me that there was a spark of remorse in him at times and that he was somewhat self-aware. But those apologies were not even close to being enough.

The next day he would be doing it all again.

Once, when I was ten years old, I let out a scream because I saw a huge tarantula as we were throwing away some honeybee hives. He was throwing one over a cliff, from this junk pile. He would throw one, then I would throw one. We got to the bottom and I picked the next one up and there was a big tarantula eating another tarantula inches from my fingers. Seeing me, it puffed up in size, so I screamed.

My adoptive dad got scared that I was scared. He was mad when he found out that I'd screamed about a spider. He therefore punched me and shoved me down on the ground because of his own reaction.

No matter what was happening, he always went to violence.

CHAPTER TEN

The Accusation

"Never try to destroy someone's life with a lie when yours could be destroyed by the truth."

—MOHAMMED SALMAN

When my adoptive parents went on a vacation one time, I stayed behind as punishment because my grades were not up to my adoptive dad's standards. He always told me that because he had made As and Bs all the way through business school, so "you shouldn't have a problem in junior high."

I stayed a week with some family friends and really enjoyed myself although it was meant as a punishment. The Hallstons were good people. They had four kids, including a daughter, Sara, who was two years old and my little buddy. She wanted to hang out with her brothers and me, but she was too small to follow us on her own, so I carried her everywhere we went.

The three kids in this family were like cousins to me as our parents were good friends. We were together very often. We went to church together regularly and they often came over to our house to use our pool. My dad even gave them a pony once. They were like family.

On this occasion, the Hallston children had all just recovered from the chickenpox and were ready to go outside and play—something I was very good at! We spent the week playing and I had a great time. While at the Hallstons', I didn't think about being a burden or a disappointment. I didn't have to worry about saying the right thing or wonder if I was forgetting to do something. I also didn't have to worry about being hurt or hiding wounds and whip marks. I just got to be me, a kid with ADHD expressing all the love in me that I could muster for everything.

During the day we would play outside, and when it got dark we would go indoors and read books, watch television, and play games together. Those are the things that kids are supposed to do. For a week, I felt free to be myself—free for the first time in a long, long time.

The Hallston kids were my pals though they were a lot younger than me. I was thirteen and they were ten and under. We had a big house with woods, a swimming pool, and lots of animals and it was exciting for them to come over, like the adventure of going to a theme park, as their parents didn't have a lot of money. My parents were well off.

One night towards the end of the week when I was staying at their house, I remember walking down the hallway toward the kitchen and I heard the mom and dad in the kitchen talking to the little girl. I walked around the corner to sit with them as I usually did at night after the younger kids had gone to bed. They stopped me before I approached the table and said, "Cody, you need to go to bed. We have to talk to Sara." So, I went back to bed not thinking much of it. The next day, the dad, a man with whom I'd always gotten along very well, was suddenly acting cold and distant. He looked at me funny at breakfast with just a stare, like he didn't know me at all. He had always been so nice to me, like a kindly uncle. Many times, we had bonded in his garage shop while he worked on his cars. I'd gone hunting with him as well.

I just sat there for a while and when he didn't talk to me I left the table. Later in the day, he said something to me like "You're a very naughty boy," which totally confused me.

I thought, *Am I? What is happening right now?* I could tell there was more to it than what he was saying. He had never been cross with me before, so his remark was unsettling.

The next day, my parents came to get me. On the way home, no one spoke, so I knew something was up. Once we were home, I knew I was in for it when my adoptive dad told me to take a walk with him and we started up the hill toward the pond with the willow tree around it. Knowing what was about to happen, because it had happened so many times before, a slow throb in my head began to sound with every other step. A familiar feeling. My head always became hot when that throb began, telling me that something terrible was about to happen. It was a mechanism of the fight-or-flight response warming up in me like an engine that only gets turned on every so often.

My adoptive dad didn't say a word, just stood at the top of the hill while I went down to the pond to climb around and find my switches—flexible sticks that he could whip me with. He had told me to pick five.

In picking switches, I tried a lot of things to make the experience easier. If I picked the wrong one, there was a good chance that I would be seriously hurt, so I had to be careful. If the switch were too big, then it would be more like a stick, and the external injuries would get me noticed at school or I would have to go to the doctor. That would make things even worse. If the switch were too small, too green, then it would cut deeply and make me bleed, and that honestly hurt worse. If it were small and too dry, then it would break, and my adoptive father would get angrier. Then I would have to pick another one. We would go from there back to square one.

I began to edge my way around the concept, not totally cognitively, of choosing the style of switches that would allow my body to deaden to the pain the quickest, while avoiding worst-case-scenario injuries. If I went with a good, medium-sized switch, giving it a lack of whip, that was not wide enough to behave like a stick, then he would be satisfied and I would be less injured, ideally.

For previous beatings, I only had to pick out one switch, so I had obviously done something extra bad this time. But I had no idea what I could've done while I was over at the Hallstons' house. My behavior was perfect from my point of view.

My adoptive parents couldn't have found something to be mad at me about in the time that they had been back, *Could they? What did I do?*

We walked from the hill to the tack room in the barn where we kept the horses. I walked in first. Standing in the middle of the tack room, my adoptive dad asked what I had done to the little Hallston girl. I didn't know what he was talking about, but my head felt like it was going to explode from the nature of that question. He made me pull my pants and long johns down around my ankles. Then he slashed at me with one of the switches and asked me again, "What did you do to that little girl?"

I guess that even when he had asked me the question the first time I knew what he was talking about. It was all the elements of what he said and did that told me that he thought I had done something sexual to Sara. As I think back on it today, I realize how awful it is for a prepubescent kid to know what he was inferring. Rape is something that children should never be exposed to, much less know with such an intimate knowledge that they can pick up an inference of it in the nuance of a statement. But you know my history of molestation and how much I had both observed and experienced first-hand while living with my mother and the Corelles. I would never have done the same to anyone. Never!

I told my adoptive father that I didn't do anything and desperately tried to reassure him of that fact, because I knew exactly what was coming. I did not want him to think this accusation of me was true, as he already clearly thought the worst of me in general.

Despite his harsh treatment of me, I also loved this man very much and wanted his respect. He taught me how to be a hard worker, how to cut down a tree and chop wood, build a barn, hunt, camp, and fish. He taught me that a job worth doing is worth doing well. I don't think I would be such a hard worker today if it weren't for him. I do believe his heart was in a good place throughout it all—even through the years of abuse. He just didn't know any better.

He told me that the two-and-a-half-year-old girl had told her parents that someone touched her privates. When her parents asked her who did, she had said my name.

I can only imagine that she said my name because she only knew a few words and I was one of her favorite people.

It was spring and I was dressed in layers. My father made me pull both layers of the shirts I was wearing up over my face so I couldn't see anything, and my arms were stuck in the air.

The beating continued and extended along the full length of my naked body. He took intermittent breaks so he could ask the same question again and so the numbness surrounding the switch marks could wear off. I could feel that my skin was starting to bleed. After a time, I had fallen to the dirty, cold concrete floor, my face in darkness under the shirts, which were now soaked with sweat, tears, and snot. I was rolling around, blindly trying to catch the lashing toward the middle of my back where it hurt less than it did on the sides and front of my body.

I heard his out-of-breath voice in the darkness while I lay on the ground naked, blinded, and bloody. "Tell me the truth. A toddler wouldn't lie about that."

By this point, I was screaming that I hadn't done anything. I could feel each impact of the switches as the wounds changed from whelps to splits to open cuts. I was rolling around involuntarily now, as his blows were whipping my sides and front. I began to wonder if I was going to die there.

Eventually all the switches were gone. I was still maintaining the truth in the hope that he would discern from my strength that I was innocent. But he picked me up, still blind and laced my body over the saddle stand. There were leather straps from the saddles and reins at hand. The beating resumed.

I began to lose my breath and it felt as if I had swallowed a bunch of chalk. My mouth was so dry that I couldn't scream anymore. I began to want to die. I called out to God to let me do just that, and this only made my adoptive father more infuriated. He made me stand up. I pulled my head through the hole in my shirt and stood as tall as I could. He asked me the question again and continued to beat me when no admission came.

He was going to keep going until I admitted to this unthinkable act. There was no way out that would stop this beating unless I gave him something he wanted: a confession.

I told him the only thing I could think of on the spot, which was that I was checking her for chicken pox. (All the kids had just recovered from chicken pox so that was a viable statement.) This was the closest thing to a confession that I could muster. Right there in that moment, admitting that I had touched that little girl when I hadn't, I was completely broken. My body was shaking and convulsing from the pain and cold.

He was sweating and had a confused look on his face. He just stood there for what seemed like forever. He was reading me to see if I was telling the truth. He never lost eye contact with me throughout his assessment of what I had just said. I wondered if he could see in my face not the fear, but the expectation that another beating was about to begin.

My teeth were chattering so hard that I thought I might have chipped one. My lower body was still exposed to the temperature of the cold March air. I watched his eyes, searching them for his reaction, and waited for what would happen. Something in his look made me think that he realized that what I had just said was the actual lie. That would mean that I had been telling him the truth all along, that he had just beaten me for an hour for no reason.

This was a man who could not ever admit he was wrong. Nevertheless, it was too late to go back. What had been done had been done and there was no way to undo it, so the easy thing for him, for his soul, was to treat the situation as if it were just.

"Put your clothes back on. We're not going to tell your mom. It would break her heart."

I hadn't fully felt what had been done to my body until I began to put my clothes back on. Until then, the adrenaline running through me must have diluted some of the pain in my system. I pulled my pants up slowly, unavoidably scraping each and every new wound from my ankles to my waist, causing blood to soak my underwear. My shirts instantly became wet and cold as I pulled them slowly back over my torso.

This was one of the worst beatings I ever endured—a beating given me for something not only that I didn't do but which I would never conceive of doing. To be accused of abusing someone else, especially given the way I grew up and what happened to me, was the worst thing that could ever happen to me. In my mind, understandably, child molesters are monsters.

We walked back out of that little room in the barn and he walked ahead of me towards the house. I walked slower and far behind him out of fear and pain, thinking at that point that anything could happen to me at the drop of a hat and for no reason.

I went straight into the house and to the shower as instructed. There, I kneeled down in the tub, staying under the warm water for as long as I could tolerate it, watching the tears, blood, and sludgy dirt running over my open wounds as they diluted into the water and went down the drain.

After I got out of the tub and had dressed, my adoptive father called me into his bedroom. My adoptive mother was there. He must've changed his mind about telling her what he thought I had done while I was in the shower. Maybe she pressed the issue and got it out of him.

"Tell your mother what you did."

From there, I had to stand in front of my adoptive mom, a woman who already strongly disliked me, and admit that I was a monster that would touch a little girl.

He then made me show her how the "truth" came to light. I turned around and slid my pajamas gently down to my ankles and lifted my shirt gently to expose my back and neck. I just stood there like that with my back to them for what seemed like several minutes. When I put my clothes on, I turned around and looked at her feet, ashamed of what I didn't do, and what had been done to me.

Would she be angry at my adoptive dad for doing this? From past experiences, I was sure that she would not. Finally, she spoke. "Cody," she said, "God created sex to be a beautiful thing between a husband and his wife."

I kept my expressionless face focused downwards. I wondered what it took for her to look at the body of a child that was as mutilated from a beating as mine was with that much ambivalence. What was it like to look at a little boy whom you are supposed to love, cherish, and protect with all of those wounds and marks on him and know that you were married to the craftsman of that torture? How could she not feel profound pity or some sort of elemental motherly instinct to protect the little boy from the monster sleeping in her bed?

"Yes ma'am," I said. Then I was sent to bed.

I never figured out what really happened or why Sara would say I touched her privates. The only thing I can think of is that a neighbor might have done something. Three or four boys would come visit their grandmother, the woman that lived in the house behind the Hallstons'. We'd all played together out in the back yard and had a great time. Those boys were the only people around us who weren't her brothers, so maybe one of them had touched her.

I would see the Hallstons at church often after this, and they even invited me back to stay with them that Christmas for a week the same year. While I was in the backseat of the car, being driven over, my adoptive parents said, "They're giving you a second chance." I myself didn't want to bring the subject up or talk about it. But my adoptive mom said, "They want you to come back and stay with them again. They've forgiven you."

The School Figures It Out

A scoliosis test. That is how school administrators finally found out that I was being whipped by my adoptive dad. I was thirteen and in line at the school. They were taking my entire class into the gym for spinal exams. My neighbor and classmate Jessica, who was standing in line next to me, knew my adoptive dad was abusive, as did most of our neighbors. Waiting in that line seemed like an eternity under the anticipation of the nurse's reaction to the story I'd made up to cover my injuries from the brutal whipping I had received in the tack room. The story I had prepared was that I was riding a four-wheeler and fell off it and into a patch of thorns. I was very anxious because I wasn't sure of the soundness of this prepared lie, but Jessica comforted me.

It was finally my turn when I got to the front of the line, I told the nurse, "Just so you know, I fell into some thorns." I thought she would totally buy it, or at least hoped she would, because I feared that I would get whipped worse if the school administrators knew the truth and if my adoptive dad believed I told them his secret. They asked me to bend over and lift my shirt, but I only got it halfway up because my shirt was stuck to my back from my still open wounds.

The nurse told me to stay right there and stepped out of the room. At this point, I was still thinking that she was believing my story. I knew from prior experience in the foster care system that if you tell an adult what has really happened, it's a gamble as they have to believe your version of events over the parents' version of events, which they rarely do. The adult at fault usually weasels his or her way out of it and then, when you get home, it's worse for you. I had been trained by other abusers to stay silent and learned that lesson well.

The nurse who had left the room came back with another nurse, and now they were both looking at my back and whispering. Meanwhile, I'm thinking, *Oh crap, I must have scoliosis.* They had me put my shirt back on after a couple minutes and said, "Okay, you can go now." So, I left, thinking my plan had worked.

About an hour later I was called to the principal's office and asked a few questions. I still stuck to my story about falling into the thorns. From the principal's office, I could see my adoptive dad standing in the hallway. They had called him. As I came out, he went into the principal's office, where he stayed for thirty to forty minutes with the door closed while I sat outside in the hallway, my heart pounding loudly in my ears.

The adults all finally came out and my adoptive dad was shaking hands with everyone and they were all laughing. He was a charming, handsome, successful man in a small town, someone everyone seemed to like. Based on how they were interacting, I thought they hadn't figured the truth out. But my adoptive dad smiled as he looked over at me and said, "Cody, you don't have to lie for me."

Years later, I found out that one of the men in that meeting was a police officer. My adoptive dad was told that if he didn't get me out of the home they were going to turn him in. He made an agreement with them that he would send me away instead of going to court. In other words, they basically swept the abuse under the rug as long as he promised to send me away.

My family counselor told me all about the place in southern Arkansas where I would be living from then on, a 150-year-old former orphanage that had been turned into a children's home run by Baptists. It was six hours away from the Renegars' house. He told me the home had horses, a pool, and lots of other cool things to do—basically suggesting that it was like an amazing summer camp.

There was such a long waiting list at the Children's Home that I had to wait for a spot to open up, so I was stuck at the Renegars' for almost another full year.

Our "Clubhouse"

During this time, me and five friends of mine who lived nearby were always trying to build our own clubhouse, but we always seemed to fail. One day we discovered an old house in the woods, and we thought it was abandoned—like a magical place had been left just for us—and we decided we would remodel it. We took down a wall, we moved some things outside to the barn, and took the chimney off the roof (sorry, Santa). We thought this was just a forgotten place and now it was ours. About a month into our "renovations," the police came knocking. That's when we found out this house belonged to an elderly couple living in a nursing home. Their grandson came by to check on it periodically. Apparently not often enough.

So, of course, I got another beating. Together we tried to explain to our parents, and I think the other ones understood more than mine did. We ended up in front of a judge who gave us a talking to (we were all sweating bullets, scared that we would be going to prison). There was a tally of the damage we had done and mine came to $4,000. To pay it off, I ended up working a project for my adoptive dad, which was clearing out a trail on our property in the woods for our horses and jeep to be able to get through. This took almost a year to do.

That's about when I was safely taken away from the horrors of the Renegar home.

Free at Last

When I left the Renegars' house, I had all Ds and Fs on my report card. I was a poor student because I was stressed out from living in a hostile environment. The effects on me were transforming my personality too. I actually found myself becoming hostile and aggressive in my thoughts. I was getting bigger and my anger was also increasing. Although I had not acted on this anger yet, I could feel it growing.

So, this removal was done with good timing! If I had stayed in that extremely violent, neglectful, and abusive home, things probably wouldn't have ended well, since I was quickly getting bigger than my adoptive dad. Who knows what would have happened if I had snapped and turned the tables on him.

If You Suspect

Not long ago, a couple of former classmates reached out to me privately to let me know how worried about me they were when we were in grade school together. I always felt so alone and had no idea anyone cared. One mentioned saying something to a teacher about seeing welts on me, though nothing came of it when he did. In hindsight, it feels good to know kids were looking out for me back then since the adults did not seem to be.

The lesson I hope teachers, students, and the parents of school-age kids would draw from the story of my life is that if you ever even suspect a child may be in trouble at home, you check. Do not make assumptions.

CHAPTER ELEVEN

From Living with My Uncle to Serving Uncle Sam

"We delight in the beauty of the butterfly but rarely admit the changes it has gone through to achieve that beauty."

—MAYA ANGELOU

Inappropriate Behavior

To save their reputation, the Renegars told everyone they knew that I was being sent to a boarding school, but they really sent me to the Children's Home in Victorville, Arkansas. Over the next four years, I gained a lot of confidence at the Children's Home. I was good with the horses, good at swimming, and a good diver. I was also great with the other kids and made many friends. Living there, I realized how powerful I can be

117

as a person and how powerful we all are. I found self-worth, my grades rose higher, and I learned a lot.

Aside from the religious aspect of life at the Home, which I did not care for, there were many good things about the Home. It really was a great place.

There were half boys and half girls there—fifty-two kids in total. During the years that I lived there, my only real problem was with Roger, the case worker who managed the boys' side of the Home. He was about forty and had exhibited inappropriate behavior with several boys, hugging them too closely and even kissing some on the mouth. When I was seventeen, he developed a crush on me and was always on the verge of sexual violation. A couple of times, he got in bed next to me and pressed his body against mine.

I hated it when he would cuddle or cross my physical boundaries, but he had a knack for walking that line. It was usually when I was upset and crying or really excited about something. This went on for two years. I was always afraid if I told on him I would be sent back to the Renegars' house, so in my mind I made excuses for his behavior. He always had a way to be completely inappropriate and yet operate well within the legal limits.

I was so starved for male attention from any type of father figure that I managed to overlook the incidents when he came into my bed because I liked the home and didn't want to make waves and be sent back to the Renegars. I felt like he was my best friend and the safest person I knew I could go to. I had a spine condition for which I had to go to the doctor once a month—and that was three hours away by car. He always drove me to the doctor and back. We had great chats about spirituality and religion on these road trips and he truly made me feel special. He told me that I had a gift to win my way into anyone's heart. I have many fond memories with him.

I had developed a sixth sense for molesters due to my early childhood experiences, but I wanted to believe Roger was a good man just being overly affectionate. He walked the line of inappropriate affection for a while and I kept telling myself that this is what a role model or father figure does when he truly loves you. Until, one day, he crossed that line.

I was crying really hard about something and since I had developed an emotional bond with Roger I went to his office to speak with him about my problem. I don't remember what the problem was, but I remember being in the embrace of a hug and bawling my eyes out when all of a sudden he had a hold of my head and put his tongue in my ear. I pulled away strongly, and as I did, he pulled my head back toward his to kiss me.

Right after I managed to pull away from him his secretary walked in and I was able to use this as an opportunity to escape. I didn't speak with Roger again for three weeks.

During those three weeks, I did some research and located a member of my birth family. I found the phone number and address of my uncle—my mother's brother—and then called him long distance. I spoke with him almost every day for a week, which I was able to do because I had quite a bit of money saved from my summer jobs. I would spend about $15 in quarters at a payphone each time I did.

From my uncle, I learned more about my family history, including all that I had missed in the years since we Dennis kids were taken away from my birth mother. And I finally told him about the guy at the Children's Home who tried to kiss me. That was enough for him to act. My uncle drove down from Oklahoma just a week after I contacted him and basically kidnapped me from the Home. Of course, I was more than willing to go with him even though it was a bittersweet moment for me. I would be turning eighteen shortly so there wasn't much that the Home's administrators could do to stop me.

My uncle took me to live with his wife and their three kids whom I got along with very well; one was just a couple years younger than me. In this house, roaches checked in and didn't check out! There were so many of them. You would turn the light on, and they would scatter. I had spent the last eight years being a preppy little rich boy, so having these pests share space with us truly bugged me. Pun intended.

I had a couple thousand dollars saved in the bank and decided that everyone in the house needed new blankets and sheets. I spent my savings on buying things to try to make the house a better, cleaner home. I had some good times there, like when I went camping with the family, among other things. But my uncle sometimes would get violent. The house swiftly became a very unstable environment for me to live in and I stopped thriving. I have pictures of me before I went there and me after being there for three months. My face and eyes were sunk in and I was so skinny because the food I was fed was not nourishing.

A lady had come to the Children's Home several times during my stay there because she was going to adopt my roommates, who were twins. She also wanted to adopt me, but I wasn't being put up for a new adoption. When she found out I was staying with my uncle roughly a thirty-minute drive from her house, she came to visit me. I looked emaciated, so she immediately packed my bags and put me in the car, saying, "You're not living here." In essence, she kidnapped me by taking me home with her.

Living with her and the twins, who, like me, were almost eighteen, I noticed she would rock them in her recliner chair. They would just lay there while she rocked. Sometimes I would walk into the bedroom I shared with the boys and she would be lying in bed with one of them with their legs intertwined. By that point, I had seen so much sexual inappropriateness that I could spot it from miles away. I got such weird vibes from her and the way she touched me that I really didn't want to stick around. Even so, I ended up being there for almost a year.

Being seventeen, I took driver's ed at school and got my driver's license. When I turned eighteen, I bought a car, a Dodge Shadow, with the money I made at my part-time job as a home health aide. I used to drive past the army base all the time on my way to work, and one day, as I drove past, I thought to myself, *Why in the world would anyone join the military?*

I mulled it over overnight and the next day joined the military. I figured it was my only option to free myself. I had answered my own question. I didn't want to stay with the sex-starved, obsessive woman or go back to my uncle's house—or god forbid, to the Renegars'. Since I was almost eighteen, I was too old to return to the Children's Home.

I needed to get away and the only escape plan I could think of was to join the army.

The Army

I went through Basic Training then on to Advanced Individual Training, where I learned auto mechanics. I was the leader of my squad and at the top of my platoon. I had worked very hard to be the best I could be and gave the army my all. Everything was going great until I was about to graduate and get a posting. But it wasn't meant to be. Apparently, I was having horrible nightmares and scaring the crap out of my roommate, a big guy, because I was screaming in my sleep.

I asked my roommate not to tell anyone because I knew that my nightmares would be an issue. I didn't even remember what those dreams were about anymore—just that when I would wake up, he would be looking over at me, concerned.

My roommate told me it was stuff from my childhood that I was screaming about. He also told our drill sergeant and the powers that be sent me to therapy. An assessment was done by the therapist, during which it was found that I was suffering from post-trauma from my childhood. All the screaming of the drill sergeants and the intense regimentation of the army procedures was adversely affecting me. It had triggered my underlying memories of abuse.

Two weeks before I was to graduate, I was discharged.

Here's a letter I wrote to Sue when I was in the army.

Dear Sue,

I'm missing you and thinking about you a lot. I thought, What would happen if tomorrow never comes? (Yes, I stole that from Garth Brooks). Like in the song, I wanted you to know how much you mean to me. Sometimes I would call you when I was so depressed I didn't know what to do. Just to hear your voice made me feel I could go on a little bit more. You mean the world to me and will always hold a big place in my heart.

I'm learning so much here. It's very interesting. Tomorrow I'm going to the gas chamber (good thing this is on army letterhead or that could be taken out of context). I'm nervous because we have to take our masks off. It's diluted tear gas. It will make my eyes and skin burn, and burn my nose, making it snotty—and sometimes this also makes people throw up.

My graduation is May 4th.

I love you,

Cody

In another letter, I wrote this:

It is hot over here and everyone has sunburn.

There are so many kinds of people here from all over the world. It's neat how we can all work together though we all come from completely different walks of life. I've had a lot of fun and a lot of not-fun here. Today our drill sergeant yelled in my face. Like right in my face. I was fighting back tears for an hour. It brought all those feelings from living with Mr. Renegar back.

I'll write again soon. Love you all, don't you forget it.

Your brother,

Cody

Army life was very hard, both drab and emotionally challenging. There's absolutely no color to be seen anywhere and for someone like me, who is highly creative, that kind of setting can be suffocating. My early years on the road with my mom and my siblings had taught me to look for beauty wherever I could find it, however, and this gave me a method to be more resilient. While doing my short stint in the army, I did my best to find beauty in the smallest forms.

I remember sitting in the grass with my platoon waiting for our drill sergeant to call on us and I found a dandelion. Because I had not seen anything beautiful in a long time, that dandelion was all I needed to keep going that day. I just stared into it for a long time, seeing the true and epic beauty in such a basic thing. It may sound simplistic, but truly it got me through that moment. Any time I saw a dandelion in the grass or on the side of the road, or just anywhere, it fueled me and reminded me of the beauty in the world. It brought back the lesson my mother had unknowingly taught me when she would put flowers in those old coffee cans.

My army experiences also reminded me of how strong I was. Even though I was discharged, I was still stronger physically and mentally than most of the people I was in training with. I had often felt weak and beaten down by my circumstances, but the army proved to me that I was neither of those things.

Except for the nightmares from my childhood that were dislodged during training, the rest of my army experience was just fine. The last thing my drill sergeant said to me as I walked out of his office was, "Too bad we're losing you. The army needs more soldiers just like you."

CHAPTER TWELVE

Choosing a Career

You know you are on the right path when you are scared to death.

Early Jobs

After my discharge from the army, I procured a job as a river guide in Colorado. I wanted to do that as a career and was on my way to do exactly that—it was my dream. I was all set to start a new life, then my "on and off again" junior high school girlfriend, Cindy, from the Children's Home, phoned me in an extremely emotional state. She cried as told me she was pregnant with the baby of a former roommate from the Home. We had never made love and I was a virgin, so it was clear the baby was not mine. Also, I was in Colorado and she was in Arkansas, and it's impossible to be hundreds of miles apart and make a baby.

She was upset because the administrators of the Children's Home were planning to send her away to an unwed mother's camp, with the intention of persuading her to put her child up for adoption. They were trying to take the choice out of her hands. Hearing this, I turned around and went back to Arkansas.

I sold the Volkswagen bus that I had intended to live in and with the cash from the sale bought a little family-sized sedan. I went back to the Home and kinda kidnapped her. I say "kinda" because she was fully consenting. Because she was almost eighteen, the headmaster didn't try to stop her from leaving.

We rented a little place on Cherry Street and basically started "playing house." We were very happy. Then, sadly, three months into her pregnancy, Cindy had a miscarriage. We mourned the unborn baby whom we had named Beau Cameron.

We had been planning to get married, and since the ball was already rolling, we went ahead with the wedding. Shortly after we married, Cindy conceived again. Our son, Levi, was born nine months after that. I had just turned twenty and she was eighteen.

Back when I was still in junior high school and living at the Home, my class took field trips to a local nursing home where we would sing and put on puppet shows for the elderly residents. After the show, we would go from room to room and chat with these folks personally. I loved doing this so much that after graduating high school, I had continued doing it on my own. I was there so often that when I turned eighteen they had to give me a title for insurance purposes. Because I would keep everyone happy, my title was "Morale Booster."

I really benefitted from the experience. I would go in and listen to these wonderful elderly people just talk and talk for hours, and think, *What a great source of wisdom.* I asked them what advice they had to give someone like me who was just starting out in life. They then would go on for hours as I soaked up information. I had never had grandparents that I knew, so I loved these exchanges and I gained so much from these visits.

Once one of the ladies at the home asked me what I wanted to do as a career. I told her that I didn't really know just yet since I was so young. She told me to write everything I could think of that I wanted out of my job and my life on a piece of notebook paper, then to fold this up and put it in my pocket. Any time I heard of a job, I was to pull out that piece of paper and read it to see if it matched the things on my list.

Now that Cindy and I were expecting a baby, finding a good job was urgent. So, I tried this technique! I pictured all the things that I wanted in a job and all the things I didn't want. The things that I wanted included working with people, doing something artistic, working with my hands, and having no limitations on the financial possibility. Any time I went into a place of business or passed a billboard or anything else that triggered the thought that maybe that was what I might want to do, I would pull out my list. Sometimes I would open the Yellow Pages and look for different types of jobs and then compare them to my list. Wherever I would go, I would pull my list out.

About two months after making this list, I went to get my hair cut. Afterwards, I got back in my car and looked at my list. Barbering checked every single box on it! I drove straight from there to a barber school and enrolled.

That lady's advice changed my life. I will be forever grateful. I've now been cutting hair for twenty-five years and I love my profession.

My barber instructor pulled me aside one day and said, "Cody, you have a natural talent. You can either take this and soar with the eagles or stay on the ground and squawk with the rest of the chickens." I realize now that what he said might be considered insulting by someone who has chosen a more traditional path. Even though I don't agree with his metaphor, his words resonated with me intensely, so I aimed high and sought more advanced training.

Upon completion of advanced barber training, the school administrators told me I had such a natural talent for cutting hair that I should learn to do women's hair also. So, I started taking courses in women's haircutting after I graduated, although I was still just planning to work as a small-town barber. I hadn't realized how far this industry goes until I got into it and learned that not only could I shoot for the moon and the stars, but I could change my stars in the process.

I just never stopped. I would keep going till I got where I wanted to be.

My First Salon

I had just turned twenty when I got a job at Jim Dancer's Hair Masters, a salon/barber shop in a small shopping center in Rogers, Arkansas. They had called the barber school I was enrolled in and asked for recommendations. My instructors told them I was about to graduate and was among the best of their students. Hearing this, they met with me over lunch. I was hired straight out of school. Cindy and I moved to a town about an hour north of where we had been living and our son was born a few weeks before I started.

I hadn't learned how to do coloring or anything yet. When I got to Jim Dancer's, I was told I should focus more on women's hair since they recognized that I had a talent for that. One of the ladies that was a stylist there took me under her wing and taught me. Another lady there, who had been working there for about twenty years, said to me, "I hope you're not planning on supporting your family with just this job. You can't live off of this. You should get a second job or something." Well, that was food for thought.

I had just finished school, and this was going to be my lifelong career and a means to support my new wife and newborn baby. At first, my coworker's words took the wind out of my sails and caused me to sink deeper into the couch that I was sitting on. I sat there for a brief moment, feeling completely discouraged, wondering if I had to get a second job as a waiter or take a new career path entirely. But my Cody instincts then quickly kicked in and I decided to use her negativity to fuel my fire and focus even harder on my goal of success.

I decided to get more advanced training.

I left that salon that day after being there for only two short months. It was, after all, a barbershop and I didn't want to exclusively barber anymore.

I got a new job at a salon called Main Street Styles in Bentonville. It looked just like the house in the movie *Steel Magnolias*, an old farmhouse that had been turned into a salon. All the ladies working there took me under their wing. I was doing roller sets on the great grandmas of the town, taking classes on weekends, and doing whatever I could to get better and better at cutting, coloring, and styling hair while raising my son. I created a magnetic energy in the salon and my reputation in the town built up very quickly. The who's who in northwest Arkansas began coming to me for haircuts and after a couple years, I was recruited by the top salon in that area, Esthetiques!

Esthetiques was an Aveda lifestyle day spa. That day spa in that small town brought in over $3 million per year! We were really doing something right and had an amazing team. The management of the salon sent me to the Aveda Cosmetology Institute in Minneapolis, Minnesota, where I did even more advanced training and became a cutting director. From then on, part of my job was to travel around the country to other Aveda salons and teach the cutters new, more advanced techniques.

Fast forward to a few years later, after a divorce from Cindy, when I was twenty-six living about thirty minutes away from her. Our son, Levi, was about six and spending weekends, holidays, and the summer with me. Then, I was flown to California for three days to work a hair show and teach a class. I quickly fell in love with Los Angeles. When the visit was over and I was sitting on a plane heading for my next training in a state where the temperature was two degrees, I became fully aware of the always perfect weather in Los Angeles. A voice in my head began screaming, *Why am I leaving this place?*

Three weeks later I sold everything I had and moved to California. I knew to reach the pinnacle of my career I could do it in Beverly Hills. So that's where I wanted to go.

California, Here I Come

Cindy agreed to let Levi come live with me in California once I was settled. I began preparing a home for us. During that time, he would come to visit me, and I would fly back to Arkansas to visit him too. At this point, my son was in first grade. Every night, over the phone, I did homework with him and tucked him into bed.

Shortly after moving to Los Angeles, I decided to do the "When in Rome" thing—or "When in Hollywood," as the case may be. I took some acting classes, did some modeling, and secured my first big break as an uncredited silent background actor referred to in the script as Cute Boy #1. The film was *Edmond,* and I was in the bar scene with William H. Macy and Julia Stiles. I had to sit at a table for eight hours pretending to eat and miming dialogue. I chose the only words I cared to say over and over again in honor of my son. For eight hours, I simply mouthed the phrase *I love Levi* over and over.

Levi now has the DVD of the movie where he can always see me saying just that any time he wants.

I applied for a job as a stylist at the well-known Beverly Hills salon owned by and named after the famous José Eber. I had gotten my California stylist license by then after being retested. I made the exact same score I got in 1996 right when I graduated from salon school. Back then they made the process of transferring from one state to another harder. Now, you just pay $60 to transfer your license.

I got my resume together, Googled the top ten salons in L.A., and decided I wasn't going to apply to any except the very best. My whole life, I always aim for the best. Everything I read said José Eber was the best, so I sent my application straight to the top. I did three interviews and demonstrated three processes: a straight razor cut, a woman's blowout, and a woman's cut. They hired me and gave me my own private room with a window above Rodeo Drive where I could look out, and they put my chair right next to the chair of José Eber, one of the most famous hairstylists in the world!

California, Here I Go

One day while working for José Eber he said to me, "You will be famous within one year. I've called it every time." Quite the compliment. I fully believed that because within the time I had been working with him I had represented the salon on countless red carpets at elite Hollywood parties bursting with A-List talent. My clientele already included Farrah Fawcett, Liz Taylor, and many other household names.

After we finished our conversation, I went back into the salon with my head held high and full of hope. My next client was a beautiful local girl. Her appointment was to have a blowout for her eighteenth birthday. This girl was born and raised in Beverly Hills, where I had planned to finish raising my son. And I said, slightly joking, just trying to make conversation, "It's your eighteenth birthday. Now you can get a fake I.D. and go to bars or get into eighteen-plus clubs." In my ignorance, I assumed that was every teenage girl's goal.

She replied with an astonished look on her face, "I've been to rehab twice and I'm currently trying to get my life back together." She was only eighteen!

When she said those words, my next thought was, *I can't raise my son out here by myself. I can't afford a nanny, I don't have family support, and I can't afford private school, all the things it's going to take to protect him.* I don't recall talking that much more to the girl after that because I disappeared into my own thoughts.

After I closed her ticket and she left, I went back and found José, who had just told me I would be famous within a year just an hour before. I told him I had to leave my dream job, one most stylists would kill for. I knew I was giving up a chance of a lifetime and had zero hope of ever returning again.

When I realized I wasn't going to move my son to California, I knew there was no reason for me to stay there. Two days later, I packed everything and moved back to Arkansas.

CHAPTER THIRTEEN

Making Amends with My Biological Mom

"Forgive others not because they deserve forgiveness, but because you deserve peace."

—JONATHAN LOCKWOOD HUIE

Mom's Imagination

When I was seventeen and temporarily living with my uncle in Spiro, Oklahoma, my mother got out of rehab and began living down the street from him in a rented trailer. During this time, the two of us took a family trip back to the hometown where my mother grew up, Spoon River, Arkansas, returning to the scene of the crime, so to speak, where she was abused. She and I went for a walk during which she held my hand. As she walked, she pretended she was licking an ice cream cone. She wanted to skip, so we were skipping across railroad tracks and she retracted into a little girl voice. I looked at her and realized that this fantasy was her safe place. She had created a world in her mind about this town and painted over the truth with a glossy picture, saying how beautiful it was to be in what, to me, seemed to be an armpit of a town. She tried to take me there with her in the fantasy while I remember looking around and thinking the town was the grossest place I'd ever seen.

That town was where all the sexual abuse in her life with her dad occurred. I didn't know these details at this time but did know she had a very rough childhood with trauma.

My mother always had a vivid imagination, which she used to cope with things. During that walk, I looked right in her eyes and saw where she had to go to survive. She and I had both endured a lot. I understood that this magical place she made up was helping her survive horrid pain. Every time my mother told me a story, she tried to paint me a perfect picture.

Letter from Mom

I didn't get to see the following letter from my mom until I was a grown-up, twenty-four-year-old man. This is the letter that my mom gave to social services the day they took us away from her, which she wanted us to see when we were adults.

My dearest five children,

Mommy loves each and every one of you and I want you to be happy with your new family. If you are not happy, Mama's not happy, and I know you would want me to be happy. Keep saying your prayers and mind your new family. Please grow up to be good men and women, which I know you will. I can't write everything I want to say, but remember, when you are adults we will talk. You be good and don't forget to remember I love you all.

Love and never ending Mama

P.S. I will always be here for you.

The Breakdown of the Letter

I will now decipher the letter and some of the underlying meaning. My thoughts are in parentheses and non-cursive.

- *I want you to be happy with your new family* (she's trying to send a coded message)
- *If you are not happy, Mama's not happy, and I know you would want me to be happy* (this comes from that little selfish place in her. Knowing my mother, it's a slight threat. She's saying, "You know you want me to be happy because when I'm not happy, I beat the crap out of you")

- *Keep saying your prayers* (the only prayer that we said, once in a while, was "Now I lay me down to sleep/I pray the Lord my soul to keep." That's the only prayer we ever did because my mother wasn't religious at all. She's trying to paint a wholesome picture for social workers who would read the letter)
- *But remember, when you are adults we will talk* (This was her way of telling us to come find her)

Today this letter reminds me that I miss her and love her. Right before she died, she spent two months with me when she came to stay on my little farm in Arkansas. I think my ability to forgive her came from my capacity to understand what she had endured in her own life. Whenever I looked at anyone that was hurting us, I knew they were broken people, so I never blamed her. My sisters, however, were very angry that she allowed so much horrible stuff to happen to them as children and it made them very bitter.

It would be easy just to blame my mom for how she failed her children. But honestly, she was very young when she had her babies and her mind had been twisted by her father and uncle. I don't think my mom had the mental capacity or intelligence to rationalize any of her behavior. I see what she was doing in the wording of the letter, even how she was being a little manipulative, and I love reading it.

In a way I blame her, and she earned that blame, but I never held the events of my childhood against her. I have always known that she didn't know how to get past the pain of her own childhood. Now that I am older and wiser, I can say, more eloquently, that she didn't know how to break the cycle of dysfunction in her family. She didn't even know she was in a damaging cycle. She didn't know she could change her stars.

Perhaps if she had read a book like this one, it might have helped her.

When I moved out of the Children's Home in Victorville and in with my uncle, I had wanted to get in contact with my mom but had no contact info for her. I had no idea where she lived or what her phone number was. Without my knowledge, he told her I was trying to get in touch with her and the next thing you know I got a letter she mailed me from rehab. It started out, *"My beautiful, brown-eyed boy . . ."*

I didn't know if my mother was going to want to see me. I didn't know if she had started a new life or had a new family, but the letter also said, "I'm so glad you contacted me." Technically, I hadn't contacted her, but my uncle told her I was trying to.

Mom Learns to Accept Her Gay Son

When I was seventeen and living with my uncle, I was being silly with my cousin and we were pretending to be very effeminate, just goofing around. My mother walked in and saw us and said something like, "I didn't give birth to no faggots." Ignorance and a prejudiced mentality like this one usually go hand in hand. Maybe I was already thinking at that time that I might be gay. But I didn't really understand what I was yet, and I had not yet labeled my sexuality. When she made this remark, I thought to myself something like, *If I were gay, I would definitely not tell that lady.*

About five years later, I took Mom to a gay bar. She had on her knee-high boots and was having a blast. I looked over and my friends were swinging her around on the dance floor. As I sat at a table after dancing, she came running off the dance floor all sweaty and out of breath and she said, "I don't care that you're gay anymore, 'cause you're so good at it." That was so validating.

She ran right back and joined my buddies on the dance floor. My friends had a blast with her. She was a little tiny thing, and they were just swinging her around.

Years later when I came out to my uncle, he said, "Don't be gay, just be bi."

Mom Stays with Sue

My sister Sue was about five months pregnant with her son and her daughter was two years old when she got a phone call at work from the Department of Human Services in Oklahoma, who had tracked her down. A DHS worker told her that our younger sister Sheila (nine) and brother Scott (six), two more kids that my mom had given birth to after we were taken from her, were at a hotel with our mother. These were children we had known of but never met. Apparently, men were going in and out of the hotel room and the kids were being locked out of the room and neglected. Law enforcement was going to take the kids away, and they would go into the foster care system unless Sue agreed to come get them. They thought she might agree because she was their biological sister.

DHS knew of Sue because our older sister, Nina, had run away from her adoptive home years before, found our mother, and given our contact information to her. I guess our mother had passed this along to the authorities.

After receiving this distressing phone call, Sue got in her car and drove to rescue our young brother and sister and learn what was going on with our mom. She took her best friend, Miranda, along with her for support.

When they got to the motel room, our cousin Jason was there with my mom. When we were younger, he used to molest her and Nina, so as soon as Sue saw him, she knew who he was. She was terrified. She was twenty by then and had her best friend with her, so she went in and gave our mom a hug and asked where her brother and sister were. Our mother said they were outside, somewhere—she didn't know. Apparently, Jason had picked mom up at the rehab clinic and brought her directly to the hotel to get drunk.

Even though the authorities were there, Jason tried to attack Sue and Miranda in the hotel room. He approached them like he was going to rape them. But they pushed him into the bathroom, where he fell into the bathtub, and escaped. They immediately told the police what happened, and he got arrested.

Our mom allowed the kids to go with Sue. But she needed a place to go herself so Sue called Nina and asked if Mom could stay with her. Nina agreed. Sue drove with Mom and the kids to our sister's house, dropped Mom off, getting there about midnight, then drove all the way back to her own house two hours away. The DHS in Oklahoma told Sue that she could not legally get custody without going to court but since our mom gave her permission to take the kids with her, it gave her the right to have them and keep them, as long as Mom never contacted Sue or knew where she lived. Otherwise, any time she asked for them, she could take them back.

Sue tried very hard not to answer Mom's phone calls. Nina agreed never to let her know where Sue lived. They both kept it up for about six months. Sue doesn't remember anymore how our mom found out where she lived—maybe she trusted Mom again. She did end up coming to live with Sue at some point, staying four or five months. She also would stay with Sue a couple more times after that. Meanwhile Sue raised our new siblings alongside her own children.

When Sue was little, she called our mom Mama, but when they connected as adults she never called her

Mom or Mama, always Joyce. Once when Sue was a child, an adoption for her fell through because she refused to call the prospective adopter Mom.

She didn't call her adoptive mother Mom until she was in her thirties. She had real issues with that word. Who could blame her?

While Joyce stayed with Sue, she would just keep coming and going as she pleased, sometimes coming home drunk.

The second time Mom came to live with Sue, Sue caught her in the hallway with our little brother pushed up against the bathroom door where she was punching him in the stomach with her fist. It took Sue a minute to realize what was happening and then Sue got very physical with Joyce. Sue grabbed her by the hair, dragged her down the hall, and kicked her out of the house. Then, she called the police. Mom left and didn't come back for several weeks but then she came back with a man asking to get her two little kids back.

I was not involved in any of this because I was only seventeen at the time. For part of it, I was still at the Children's Home and then I was staying with the strange lady and in the Army.

The Apology That Never Came

As I have said, I was able to forgive our mother. I have always been able to instinctively forgive easily. I know everyone is human and we are all slightly flawed. For my sisters, however, it was a lifelong struggle to forgive our mother though they actively tried.

Eventually my mother ended up marrying another man and we were at their house all having heart-to-hearts about what happened to us growing up. Nina and Sue kept saying to Mom, "All we want you to do is say you are sorry and admit that you allowed this to happen to us." They were crying and upset because she wouldn't admit it.

According to Mom, it was always someone else's fault. She wouldn't take responsibility.

It got to the point where we all walked out of the house. After we shut the front door, I went nuts and said to my sisters, "No, we're not leaving. All you want is an apology from her." I turned around and kicked the door off the hinges and walked right up to Mom and cornered her. I said, "You did this to my sisters! You allowed that stuff to happen to them! You say you're sorry to them now. Until you apologize, we are done with you."

She still refused to apologize.

The *only* way she had survived this far was by pretending things were very different than they were. She had no sense of reality because reality was too hard for her to handle.

That was the first time my sisters had ever seen me get truly upset. I was physically shaking after that confrontation until my sisters took me out of the house and calmed me down.

CHAPTER FOURTEEN

Marriages, Divorces, and Dating

When the wind blows, open your sails.

When Cindy and I were playing house, we moved up to northwest Arkansas. I was working seven days a week trying to build a clientele and she was pregnant. Things ended up not working out after Levi was born and we decided to go in two different directions. She had known that I had experimented with guys, yet I still didn't realize I was gay. I thought I was just very "open minded" or "European." Our relationship did not end because I was gay but because we were too young and not ready for marriage yet.

I had never even really heard the term *gay* yet—or at least not so it stuck with me. I had spent most of my life that far in pure survival mode, so I hadn't had the luxury of figuring out my sexuality. I was also raised in religious situations where if I did hear anything about homosexuality, it was always in the context of a

"Sodom and Gomorrah" type sermon or something comparable. Nothing that I had heard about men loving men seemed related to me, until I got older.

The divorce from Cindy set me on a path of self-discovery. There was a period in which I dated both women and men. I concluded that I was in fact a gay man when the show *Will and Grace* came on TV. That was when I said to myself, *Oh, I think that's what I am.* That show helped me accept the side of me I was only beginning to know.

I basically raised my son on my own. Cindy moved out when he was two and a half years old and I hired babysitters to watch him while I was working. When I traveled for work he would stay with my sister Sue and her children.

Cindy got married again a couple of years later and had another child. And more recently, she had another baby with a new man in her life. She and I have remained good friends. My ex-wife has always been more like a sister to me.

When I was twenty-six I was traveling, cutting hair, and doing well with that, getting some recognition and teaching classes. That's when I was sent out to L.A. I stayed there for a couple years while Cindy took Levi to her house. But, as I've already said, I didn't want to raise Levi out there, so I moved back to Arkansas.

Back home in Arkansas, I dated off and on for a few years and then met Tony. By this time, I was in my mid-thirties. Later, we had a commitment ceremony, but we were never legally married as same-sex marriage was not legal in our state at the time.

I was ready for my "close up." I was interviewed in the documentary film *Hollywood to Dollywood* by Gary and Larry Lane. My part in the movie was kind of a tearjerker moment in the film. I got a lot of attention and they got a lot of questions at the film festivals about me. This later would lead to me being interviewed for a book called *Rainbow Relatives*. I got to speak to the author, Sudi Karatas, about my wonderful relationship with my son and how I was fighting for marriage rights. I was happy to be part of such an informative and entertaining project.

Cody, the Crusader

After the documentary was released, Yahoo sent a reporter to my house, who did a whole story on me. While the reporter was there, I was planning my wedding to Tony and I called the local newspaper to put my engagement photo in it only to be informed that it was against their policy to post same-sex marriage announcements. When I asked, "Why?" they said, "Well, that's just the way we've always done it." The reporter in my kitchen overheard this and he said, "Well, I'll write your wedding announcement!" and he did. This is still on Yahoo.

We had a big, beautiful wedding at our farm, in our garden overlooking the pond. People asked us why we didn't fly to another state where it was legal to do it. I said, "That's just jumping through hoops and just taking scraps of equality."

The announcement the reporter did kind of went viral, so his boss told him he wanted him to do a whole story on the discrimination that happened to us. That also went viral and we got thousands and thousands of messages, and we were on the news often. We became poster boys for marriage equality in Arkansas. Ellen mentioned us. *Good Morning America* and *Good Day L.A.* talked about our wedding; it was everywhere. Pretty much everyone in this little town knew about us. Even most people in the whole state and a growing number nationwide. We were part of many public events including being asked to be grand marshals in the local pride parade. Many people were suing their states over marriage equality rights at this time. Since we had created so much clout and awareness at this point, we were asked to join the Arkansas lawsuit, which we did, which launched us into an overwhelming and unfamiliar world of legal events throughout many months. A few days before our lawsuit finally went to court, we won, but we knew they were going to repeal the decision. There were many rapid-fire weddings—in fact, 950 of them.

By the time it became legal for us to marry, he had already left.

The Split

Less than a year after our ceremony, I bought Tony a piano because I knew taking lessons was a big deal when he was a kid, and he was always talking about picking up the piano again. I was on my way home when I called to tell him about the surprise and he said, "Cody, don't have the piano delivered, I want to tell you something when you get home." I had no idea what was about to happen. I got home and found him sitting at the dinner table with his suitcases packed. He began to tell me that his heart was now elsewhere, he'd met someone new, and explained that he wasn't in love with me any longer. I remember having tunnel vision. The biggest irony was that we had finally won our case for marriage equality and now I was single.

I was just sitting there when he was ending his story to tell me he was leaving and I instinctively thought, *Okay, first thing, I'm going to have to heal. It's a process I know well. Boy, the universe sure has a funny way of letting you know you are not where you are supposed to be and it is telling me I'm done here. I came, I did what I had to do, my son is grown, people can get married. Wow! So, what's my next adventure?*

One thing for certain, my life has taught me was how to heal. What do you do when someone says they don't love you anymore? I wished he would hurry up and go.

Of course, I was still in love with him. This was occurring just shy of a year since our wedding. I knew I would have to grieve because it was basically a death. But I told him, "I wish you the best. Good luck. You guys go do your thing."

I wasn't going to beg him to love me. There are eight billion-plus other people on this planet, why would I beg anyone to love me?

As soon as he was gone, I did what every heartbroken guy or gal does. Ate horrible food, laid on the couch and cried, drank too much wine, and watched sad movies. After many weeks of doing that, one day I just literally told myself, "Okay, that's enough. You have to just stand up." I hadn't gone back into our bedroom since the breakup. I was sleeping on the couch in the living room. Now, I looked at my feet and said, "Walk. Just put one foot in front of the other," and then I forced myself to do just that, and to breathe consciously, shower, and go outdoors and into the sunlight.

As my mood improved, I became excited about what the universe had in store for me in the next chapter of my life. I started exercising, riding my mountain bike around our local lake every day. There were deer and rabbits and turtles everywhere, and I was surrounded by beauty.

With every breath I took, I had to choose happiness again. Sometimes I would break down crying at random moments. Maybe I would be driving down the road and have to pull over, maybe while I was eating breakfast or watching television. I knew this was all part of the mourning process and I embraced it wholeheartedly.

The only thing that can heal this type of pain is time. It is a must to grieve and grieve with all your might; and then you must stand up and dust yourself off, even if you don't think you are quite ready. Don't let yourself stay in that dark place forever. Know when it's time to burn bright again.

Six months later, I went on a gay cruise and never looked back.

A Break from Dating

After my divorce, I took a two and a half-year hiatus from dating. I knew a relationship was not what I needed. Up until that point, I had been in four long-term relationships, each lasting at least three years. I was like a serial long-term dater. My relationship with Tony had lasted six years.

While reflecting, I concluded that I needed to do something differently. They say if you keep doing the same thing over and over again while expecting different results, then you're crazy. I don't know that I was quite doing the same thing over and over, but there had to be something I was doing wrong, because I kept finding myself single and I was approaching forty quickly. I figured the only thing that I wasn't doing was focusing on myself.

Each of my relationships had failed for the same reason: my partner was cheating. So, if I was dating the same kind of guy over and over and expecting different results, maybe I needed to change my type or upgrade my standards—or change my stars. After that breakup, I thought, *I can't go through another one.* I realized I needed to get to know myself better, to kind of date myself for a bit. So, I took myself to dinner, did things I wanted to do, and delved into what I really wanted. I also traveled by myself, took camping trips by myself, and did lots of other things.

That doesn't mean I was celibate. I'm not that crazy. I just didn't date.

I had to look at things about myself very closely to get to know myself better. What I found out is that I was horribly impatient, whereas I had previously believed I wasn't. I found out I had abandonment issues, which seems like it would be obvious, but it wasn't to me. I understood where those came from once I realized I had them. Because of the abandonment issues, I would become extra clingy or overanalyze things, and I was probably smothering my partners because of that fear.

I was so scared that people were going to leave me that I would unconsciously push them away, which then became a self-fulfilling prophecy. Once I found that out about myself, once I actively found the origin of these flaws, then I was able to shut them down. I told myself that I could and would survive the worst-case scenario. That it didn't matter who left me or who stayed, no matter what I would always be 100 percent whole and continue to choose happiness.

I knew if I listened to my heart and to the energy inside me, the answers I was seeking would be there. I just had to find them. And, holy crap, it was true. They were there the whole time. When I felt ready to date, I met my husband, Terry, within a few weeks on Tinder. But I didn't go on a date with him for a couple months. I finally agreed to the date after he sent a video of himself smiling and laughing and I knew I wanted to be a part of that happiness.

CHAPTER FIFTEEN

Fighting for and Raising My Son

*"It's up to us to break generational curses. When they say,
'It runs in the family,' you tell them, 'This is where
it runs out."*

—LORI DESCHENE, *TINY BUDDHA*

Raising Levi

When Levi was young, Levi's mom and her boyfriend decided they were moving to North Dakota and took my child to North Dakota for three months! Cindy had legal custody—a court in Arkansas would never give custody to the dad. So, I had to execute a plan to get him back with her consent.

I got a tiny house that was perfect for raising my boy. It had a big yard where I put up lots of rope swings and there was room for our many pets. I prepared the home perfectly, not even knowing if my plan would work. One thing I did know about Levi's mom is that she desired money and I was able to use her desire to my advantage. Originally the court ordered me to pay her $350 a month in child support. I had volunteered an extra $1,000 a month the first year and for the next eight years gave her $750 a month. To get her to agree to bring Levi back to Arkansas from North Dakota to stay with me, I told her I would still pay the $750 in child support even though Levi wouldn't be living with her. I even bought her a car. She brought my son back in exchange for twelve more years of child support payments.

I was lucky I could afford it. I know many parents would love to have this option. The deal ended up being worth every penny because I was able to raise Levi until he was eighteen and this was the best gift I ever gave myself. I love him so much and he grew up and became a wonderful, kind, loving, hardworking father himself.

Fighting for Levi

When I was about twelve my adoptive parents may have been figuring out that I might be gay, although it still hadn't occurred to me yet. They decided I needed an older teenage male role model in my life and had a local college guy, named Paul who was one of the church youth group leaders, start coming over regularly and riding horses with me, camping with me, and playing the role of a big brother to fill a void they thought I had that I didn't really need filled.

Cut to a few years later. Paul found out I was gay when Cindy outed me to him and the next thing I knew, Paul, this millionaire, big muscle-head and his wife, very religious people, tried to take my child away from me! Cindy, my son's own mother, almost gave my son to them, and I had to go and retrieve him from their backyard. They had three girls and I think they wanted a son. They were saying I couldn't have him. Hearing this, at first I pulled away, thinking, *These people have millions. He's physically strong and an ex-football player, I can never succeed.* I felt so helpless.

I was sitting in my parked car down the street from their house and sobbing because I didn't know what to do. I wanted to avoid an in-person confrontation. I was thinking I wasn't big enough or strong enough—or rich enough, if it came down to a lawsuit—to get him back. As I sat in my car, my sister Sue instinctively knew to call me and ask, "What's wrong? What's happening?" I told her Paul had my son and wouldn't give him back. Hearing this, she said, "Go get your son," then talked me through it.

Stealthily, I pulled up near their house. I heard the kids playing in the backyard. I walked around the corner and saw the two grownups standing on the other side of the yard, and the kids were playing on the swing set. I walked over and as quietly as I could, picked up my son, who was three years old, and he hugged me tightly. I turned right around, walked off with him in my arms, strapped Levi into his car seat quickly, got in, and left. If Paul had seen me, he probably would have tackled me, and this story would have ended differently.

A Kid Needs Space

When Levi was thirteen he rode a motorcycle to school every day. With very little property, he didn't have anywhere else to ride it, so he rode it into the tiny house and through the living room and kitchen, and out the back door. Seeing this, I thought to myself, *I've got to get this kid some land.*

I immediately picked up my phone and called my friend who is a realtor. The next day, we started looking at houses. We looked at many properties that didn't fit what I was looking for. My friend told me that the house I wanted at the price I wanted didn't exist, but I knew it was out there. I wanted a small farm with some property where Levi could roam with enough room to keep animals that would be a healthy place for him to grow up. It took me about a month to find the place I had visualized. Though I had looked at a bunch of houses in the Ozark Mountains, I finally saw a new one that had just been listed the night before. I went down the next day and the property was exactly what I was looking for! I put down an offer right then and we lived there for the next four years.

Levi and I immediately went to work turning the house into our home. We painted the outside and the inside. We built beautiful shutters for all the windows and a wraparound deck. We put up a cute little red barn and a big chicken coop together. Outdoors, we planted an orchard and a big garden, and we populated the yard with fainting goats, which are goats that literally faint when they get startled. Very funny to watch. You can see some on YouTube videos if you have not yet witnessed this.

We also had pheasants, a turkey, and different types of exotic chickens, a pond with ducks, and two squirrels. Three dogs and a pig that lived inside were also part of the family.

Here Levi was able to enjoy being a wild boy in the country with plenty of room to spread his wings. The house was even right by a river.

Discipline

I did my best to raise my son right. To encourage and to discipline him. A good balance is key. Whenever I told Levi no, I always helped him rationalize it. I'd ask him, "Why do you think I said no?" I never was the "Because I said so" type of parent.

What I would say was, "You aren't allowed to argue but you are allowed to debate. You are allowed to tell me your side and I will tell you my side." I wasn't a dictator by any means. If I said no, I would make sure he understood why and that he agreed. But I would make sure he had the opportunity to disagree.

One example: When I told him that he was still too young for a motorcycle, several times to persuade me to change my mind he said, "I promise I'll be *so* careful." Then we looked at statistics of kids who had them at his age. I wanted him to be able to think for himself, so that when I wasn't around to tell him no or yes he would have the tools he needed to come up with good answers on his own.

I always made my son Levi do his homework and talked to him about college, trying to get him prepared. And anytime he would show interest in anything I would just go full force towards it. At one point, I took him to this air show and asked, "What do you think about this as a career?" and he thought that was just perfect, so we looked into flight schools. We just delved into anything he was into. Levi was always into mechanics and since I was trained as a mechanic by the army I was able to teach him a little bit. He combined what he researched on YouTube and the internet with the basics I taught him and learned to turn those skills into a way of making a living as a mechanic as an adult.

He's very transient. He has a girlfriend named Alaya and three babies. They have lived in everything from an RV to a van and bus, making what they call a "conversion van" or "boutique bus" with a kitchen area, so they can have a home on wheels and travel. They are what is known as "Van lifers." They are minimalistic and don't want much. To simplify their existence, they sold everything and bought a camper and van. They also have contagious and adventurous spirits. They have traveled all over the country and parked in national parks and campgrounds everywhere from the mountains of Colorado to the beaches of Florida.

Due to a few medical hiccups and having three kids, Levi and his girlfriend at last decided to settle down on a beautiful farm in southern Missouri. He's hard-working, has good ethics and strong morals, and is a very loving man in his early twenties. He loves cars and working on jeeps and vans. To make money and provide for his family, he builds conversion vans like the ones he himself had for customers.

It was amazing that I was able to teach him all these things even though I had nothing to guide me. When I was younger, people often asked me, "How are you able to be such a good dad when you never had a good role model or loving parents?"

I would answer, "Well, I know what *not* to do. I know what hurting feels like. I know what struggling feels like. So, I just do my best to put myself in my son's shoes." I'm an extremely empathetic person and that helped me understand him and raise him better.

Skydiving with Levi

I went skydiving when Levi was seven and he was so upset that he couldn't go with me because of the age restrictions. Ever since then he wanted to go skydiving.

When he turned eighteen, I finally took him. When he jumped out of the plane and I watched him turn into a tiny dot below me, I wanted to yell out, "Daddy's coming." He is my heart, so my heart was dropping out of the sky. I jumped out and caught up with him just before I opened my parachute. Then it was just like sitting on a swing set in the clouds, just swinging in the harness. If you pull on the toggles you'll spin, so we both pulled them at the same time.

It's so quiet up there that you can hear each other speaking. Nothing like in the movies. You could hear someone two miles away, as there's nothing up there. I called out, "Hey Levi, how ya doing?" He said, "I love this, Dad." It was really cool. This was one of the most beautiful experiences of my life.

I never wanted Levi to feel any of the pain I felt, and I wanted to be a good dad. And now he is a dad to his own kids, which makes me a very young and happy grandpa.

The greatest healing in my entire life came from becoming a father—not that anyone should bring a child into the world for any purpose other than love. For me, it just happened to be a very healing experience because the older I got the sadder I was that I didn't have father-son memories of things like throwing a ball together in the yard. I didn't have those kinds of memories and experiences in foster homes, so I was always a little jealous of kids who had those beautiful memories with their dads and moms.

Slowly, by being a dad and raising my son mostly on my own, I became like a mom as well as a dad. By this, I mean I had to be nurturing, and by nurturing him I was nurturing myself. When I threw a football with him, I was also throwing a football with my younger self. All those memories I didn't have, I was finally able to create. I was on the other side of it, the dad side, but it's still a good memory—just as beautiful and just as important.

The greatest gift I gave my son was being a wonderful dad, and the greatest gift he gave me was recreating the childhood I never got to have and seeing things through his eyes. That's just one of the many reasons I cherish my son so much.

Levi and Alaya have given me wonderful grandbabies, Hayze, Hayven, and Harli, whom I get to spoil, and I especially love that I get to be the fun guy. I'm there to guide Levi with advice. Grandbabies are my reward. I feel like they are God's way of saying he never forgot me.

CHAPTER SIXTEEN

Other Siblings and Kin

*"In some ways, siblings, and especially sisters, are more
influential in your childhood than your parents."*

—DEBORAH TANNEN

Among my five core Dennis siblings (whose last names
all became different after adoption), I had two little
brothers and two older sisters, and I was always being
pulled between the two groups. Either my little
brothers wanted to play with me, or my older sisters
did, but the older and younger ones never played
harmoniously together. I think being a middle child
taught me some good social skills and made me a good
mediator as an adult. I think I rationalize things better
and process things thoroughly because of my birth
position among my siblings.

My youngest brother was spoiled a little because he
was such a cute baby with bright blond hair. Everybody
wanted to hold him.

I was born on Marilyn Monroe's birthday. My sister Sue was born on Elvis Presley's birthday. My baby brother was born on the exact day Elvis died. And we were taken from our mother on the anniversary of the day Marilyn Monroe died.

My Sister Sue

My constant in this totally inconsistent world is Sue. I've talked a lot about Sue in this book because she is so special to me. She never left me, even when we were adopted by different parents. Also, she always has had a maternal instinct and mothered me more than anyone else. When I was in the army, she got a toll-free 800 number so I would be able to call her any time I wanted. Every step of my life, she was my foremost supporter.

I have tested everyone that has been in my life other than Sue. I've tried to push them away and if they pushed back, I knew they were going to be here for me. That's something I noticed about myself years ago, my emotional need to see if they are real. So many people in the past came into my life and said I would be safe and that they loved me and nothing else bad would happen. Soon afterward, they started beating me or abusing me in some way. Sue has been tried and true throughout. Even if we get mad at each other, she's there. Whereas my other brothers and sisters are not.

Sue also has been there for my son, Levi. She's gone above and beyond to make sure we are both okay. She's done the same for everyone else in our immediate family, but they sort of uniformly rejected her outreaches.

Sue married and later divorced the father of her two children. Today she is in a beautiful, healthy relationship. Her kids are grown, and she has three grandbabies. Recently she started building a log cabin on a beautiful mountain she bought in Arkansas. She actively cultivates a relationship with my son, her nephew, who visits her on her mountain often with his own family in tow.

When We Say Nothing at All

Sue and I have a song we think of as our anthem, *When You Say Nothing at All*, which was a hit for Keith Whitley years ago and then for Alison Krauss. The reason that this "our song" is because so many times she called me when my heart was broken and I was crying and she would say, "Cody, what's going on? Are you okay?" Somehow she just knew when to phone. I believe everybody is connected by energy and that we share a collective consciousness and also that when you are closer to someone the energetic connection is heightened.

My sister and I are as close as siblings can get because of enduring so many years together fighting simply to survive. That experience bonded our hearts and minds. She knows my feelings before I ever even have them, and she'll call me spontaneously while I'm crying halfway across the world. I swear, there have been way too many coincidences to deny the truth of this.

Remember how Sue was driving down the road and suddenly knew that I needed help to get Levi back from Paul who took him from me? That time, she rang me just as I was dialing her.

After I got Levi back and things had calmed down, I asked her, "How did you know what was up with me?" She said she knew it in her heart.

It has always been like that. We know what the other is thinking sometimes.

Sue was married to a man that was abusive. He was a bodybuilder and a big man, but I stood up to him once and called the police when he and Sue were at my house. Sue was sitting in a chair and I was seated across from her on the couch. We locked eyes and exchanged a mental message with each other about the cop. Then, we busted out laughing. We were both making fun of the cop in our heads, just looking at each other not saying a word.

Coming Out to Sue

Before I was married and had a kid, Sue asked me if I was gay. I said no because at that time, to the best of my knowledge, I wasn't. I hadn't even pondered my sexuality.

I found out that her hairdresser had asked her if I was gay and she'd said no. But then she started observing me closer and thought, *Holy crap, he is!*

Although she informed me I was gay, I kept saying, "No, I'm not."

She was like, "Okay, we'll wait and see."

As I matured, I began to realize there might be some truth to her words and it turned out she knew me better than I knew myself. When I was twenty-two, I invited Sue and our older sister, Nina, to my house. They knew I was going through a divorce. I explained to them that I wanted to be able to share my life with someone who loved me unconditionally and wanted to live happily.

Sue was elbowing our sister, "He's finally gonna come out," and Nina was like, "No, he's not."

When I said, "I'm gay," Sue said, "Oh my God, I knew it!" Then she turned to Nina, saying, "See, I told you he was gay and ready to come out." Sue knew already and didn't care, except about my happiness. She said, "What does it matter?"

Sue has marched in Pride Day parades with me and her daughter, Samantha, once marched with us when she was eight months pregnant. Sue was supportive when I came out to her. I think I had been slowly showing her because when I came out, she also said, "Well, it's about time." That very night we went to a gay bar together.

At the same time, Nina said, "Although I don't agree with your lifestyle, I'll support it."

Sue often would go with me out to the gay clubs in our town. She didn't want me to be on my own, doing stupid stuff, so she was kind of my bodyguard, making sure I was okay. She also did fiercely chase off a few guys because they were not behaving properly.

The Greatest Gift My Sister Ever Gave Me

My sister's daughter, Samantha, has been a familiar spirit since the moment she arrived on this planet! I was fifteen when she was born and knew immediately that we were going to be great friends! We are so much alike. We've always shared a passion for books, musicals, magic, and pretty much anything shiny! One of my favorite memories was surprising her with Britney Spears concert tickets when she was ten years old and taking a road trip three hours away to Little Rock, Arkansas. We had the best time and made enough memories in that one weekend to last a lifetime.

I have always been very picky about the people that I bring into my life, but this beautiful soul just found her way right into my heart from the start without even knocking. She is now a wonderful mother herself.

My relationship with my niece is a true treasure. I could not have asked for a more loyal sidekick.

The Other Siblings

My little brothers Randy and Charlie were unfazed by the news that I was gay. Frankly, they were so strung out on drugs and had their own issues to deal with to give a damn about me. In fact, a couple months after I came out to them, one of my brothers stole my brand-new car and wrecked it. The police were called, and we found him hiding in my closet with a butcher's knife. I didn't end up pressing charges. My two brothers were always acting like the two stupid guys in *Dumb and Dumber.*

Nina, Randy, and Charlie always seemed to be a little jealous after we were separated into different homes because I was adopted by "rich people." After we were put into our different new families, my brothers were put into middle-class families where they didn't have as much money. Sure, I got adopted by a family that was extremely wealthy, but my brothers and sisters didn't know about the dark reality I was facing on a daily basis. They were envious because they were unaware of the harsh beatings and emotional abuse I endured.

I had a conversation with one of my brothers recently and he said something about me being lucky to be raised by the Renegars. I said, "Did you know that my adoptive dad was beating the shit out of me?" Maybe Sue did say something to my brother about this years earlier, but he didn't remember. He'd always been very focused on himself.

He also complained to me that he was a victim of the State. To which I replied, "No, you are a victim of no one but yourself. You are a victim of you."

I believe we can't just go through life mad at everyone who has done us wrong, as that perpetuates a never-ending cycle. Don't waste time blaming your stars, just change the stars.

I think my brothers might have felt it was like being adopted was a competition. It is ironic that they were envious of me because their families were very nurturing and loving.

Like so many other people who like to play the victim, my brothers seemed to blame everyone else instead of being accountable for their own shortcomings. They are now in their forties. One time when they were visiting my house I overheard them saying to each other, "We could have this too."

I said, "That's the point! You can have this too!"

Letting people know they can change their circumstances is one of the biggest reasons for me wanting to write this book. Everyone can have all this. Anyone can have whatever I have and a million times more. I'm satisfied with everything. Yes, I'm ambitious, but ambitious for happiness and not at all ambitious for money. By contrast, my brothers seek money for happiness and end up in and out of prison and probably always will.

My brothers went to prison for selling drugs, mostly. They were together and tried to rob someone and it went wrong. One brother apparently had a cigarette lighter in his pocket and was trying to make it look like a gun through the fabric in the coat. They were drunk and the feeble robbery attempt was not successful, but they were sent to prison anyway, mostly for breaking their probation by being publicly intoxicated.

Another time, they got pulled over for a taillight out. They hadn't done anything illegal, but they were so used to running from the cops that they jumped out of the car out of habit and took off running toward the woods by the side of the road. One of them fell off a small cliff and knocked himself out. He woke up lying in the dirt the next day. So, he managed to evade the police.

The other brother was arrested.

They ran and yet they didn't need to run. They had done nothing wrong; it was just a knee-jerk reaction.

I knew both of their adoptive families fairly well. They were very nice, very attentive, very engaging people. In my opinion, what their adoptive parents did wrong with my brothers is that they never told them no. Their new parents couldn't have children of their own so when they finally were able to adopt they were overly indulgent. It's definitely not good parenting.

I think it comes from guilt. The parent wants the kid to have such a good, happy life and they think saying no is something negative. But no is so necessary for structure, for positive reinforcement, and for guiding your child. If they say no, they think they are depriving them somehow. But they are really depriving the child of a healthy future.

The boys couldn't say no to drugs and the parents couldn't say no to the boys. As a result, my brothers are felons.

Just because we have the same mother doesn't mean I have to be friends with them. I didn't want my son around them. They have both been in and out of prison since they were twenty and are bad influences in every way. One was homeless the last time I checked and the other went back to jail again in 2020. On his Facebook page, he posted that he had made a "poor decision" just before going back to prison.

No matter the amount of people or teams of support that one has, the blaring reality always rears its ugly head. You ultimately and absolutely cannot help people who won't decide to help themselves.

Just because someone is blood-related to you doesn't mean you need to have them in your life. If they are toxic for you for any reason, you may have to decide on a safe distance between you or cut ties altogether.

My Older Sister Nina

I concluded a while ago that my relationship with Nina was an unhealthy part of my life. Ever since then, I have kept her at a safe distance. We text a little or message on Facebook. But it seems like we speak two different languages. I want to be a light for her children, to set a good example for them. I've always wished this for all my brothers and sisters and their children.

One of the driving reasons for writing this book is to show members of my family who had the same rough start as I did that they could walk a path towards happiness and don't have to live in a victimized state of mind. With every tiny or big choice made in life, they can consciously choose life and happiness. The same is true for you and me.

Like any muscle, the more often you use the choosing muscle, the stronger it gets. You just have to start.

CHAPTER SEVENTEEN

Reconnecting with My Biological Dad and Closure with My Adoptive Dad

"I would like to thank every person who has ever been unkind to me. You taught me to be even kinder to others."

—STEVEN AITCHISON

Reconnecting with My Biological Father

I reconnected with my biological dad when I was twenty-two or twenty-three. When I found my biological mom at eighteen, she told me that his name was Jerry Dennis, but that's all the info she could give me except his birth date. This was back in 1998, before the internet, Facebook, and Google searches. In the back of the printed phone book was the map of the United States, and every state had its own set of area codes. I literally just started calling each directory assistance number to look him up and other people whose last names were Dennis. I knew he was in southern Texas at one time, so I started there. I would only do a certain amount of calling every month because I was on a budget, working a lot, and I only had a certain amount to spend on calling 411 for information, which quickly racked up quite a tab.

I must have called hundreds and hundreds of numbers. I probably ruined a few marriages because when someone would answer, I would say, "I might be your son," and they'd hang up on me. I was hung up on multiple times. I knew my mom called him Gerald, but I didn't know if he went by Gerald or Gerry or Jerry or Jay, so I looked for every variation I could think of and spent hours each week doing that.

Finally, after about a year, the right guy answered the phone. I said, "I think I'm your son" and he asked, "Is this William?" I thought, *Who the hell is William?!* That's when I found out we had two additional older brothers I had never known about. (These men were born ten years before my dad met my mom.) Jerry drove down from Illinois a week later and Sue and I met him on Father's Day in 1998. He was in his late seventies when we reconnected. We learned he'd been married for over twenty years to his second wife and had four more boys with her.

That day we went for a boat ride on a lake. Jerry came down a couple more times, and Sue and I went up to Illinois and met our new brothers and Jerry's wife. Our biological dad was a jolly little man with a pot belly and a contagious laugh. A truck driver for years, he loved to tell stories. We didn't really have a lot in common and I couldn't understand the way he spoke. He was wearing dentures but apparently had thrown the bottom ones away. In fact, nobody could understand him because of his missing teeth and his really thick local accent, but once he started laughing everyone laughed with him. Hearing us laughing seemed to prompt him to tell another story.

One day, I got this message from a lady in Texas who said, "Hey, I think you're my cousin."

Then she explained how her father was Jerry's brother and went on to tell me that she used to babysit me. During that conversation, I found out that this side of my family had been trying to find me and my siblings since I was ten months old and my mother left our father.

My newfound cousin told me that I was given the middle name Cody in honor of her dad's favorite horse. She also sent me a bunch of pictures, some of our grandparents and other relatives and one of me as a baby. I had never seen pictures of myself younger than five years old before. That was really something.

I felt like I found a large piece of a puzzle that I didn't even know was missing, like those pictures and finding out where I came from was filling a void in me that I didn't even know I had. Everything had finally come full circle for the Dennis family.

The Cycle of Dysfunction Stops with Me

Throughout my life, whenever a flaw in my character has presented itself, I am adamant about finding the root of it and figuring out a way to fix it. It's always been my mission to better myself and overcome personal challenges. I truly welcome these challenges because facing them makes me a better person for myself, my son, and those around me.

Because I was always painfully aware of the lack of traditions in my unusual childhood, I was set on not letting my son grow up without them, especially at Christmas. I started some traditions with Levi when he was young, including listening to Christmas carols on a record player in our matching Christmas pajamas while decorating the tree and drinking homemade cider, that we continued for years. They felt very important to me.

One Christmas, when my son was thirteen, I was trying to continue these traditions and he just wanted to eat pizza and watch TV. Aggravated, I went into a full-blown tantrum and I said, "That's not what we do! At Christmas, we should roast a duck or make a nice tree, but fine let's just throw the tree away." On and on I vented until I saw the look on my son's face and realized how angry I was coming across. He was looking at me like a deer in the headlights, holding his pizza, and his expression said, "What the hell?" like I was a complete idiot.

I quickly realized my reaction had nothing to do with him. He was doing nothing wrong and I was scolding him. I just stopped in my tracks and apologized profusely to him, "Levi, I am so sorry for what just happened right now," I said, "We can eat pizza. That can be our tradition. Let's eat pizza and watch TV every year." Since then, we have had many more magical memories at Christmas that he still looks back on fondly.

After my apology, I gave him a hug and told him I had to go make a phone call. Right after my rant/breakdown with Levi, I went and called my adoptive dad, whom I had not spoken to in twelve years. It was 10 PM and he was in his seventies at this point, so it was past his bedtime. I woke him up. I said to him, "We are meeting tomorrow for breakfast. I have issues and this recent issue just affected my son, so, we are meeting for breakfast tomorrow."

I continued, "You are the only one who can help me through this because I'm very upset with you, very hurt." I was upset about what I lost. He and I could have had such a beautiful relationship, but I did not know how to jump over the hurdle of feeling wounded by him.

I guess calling him was kind of like that thing people do in AA where they call people to make amends for the ways they hurt them, except I was calling him to give him an opportunity to make amends to me for the ways he hurt me. Meeting with him felt to me like it would be the only way I could get through this newly presented flaw so that my son and I would never have that kind of experience again.

The phone call that night to the man who adopted me so long ago led to our breakfast meeting the next morning. The both of us sat down over coffee and slowly talked about my childhood and all the things that happened to me. He listened quietly, with tears streaming down his face, as I resurrected the years of abuse I suffered. I concluded by describing my memories of the worst beating he ever gave me over the little girl. He sat there with tears in his eyes, obviously trying to work up the strength to speak, and when he finally did, he simply whispered, "I don't remember any of that."

My reaction was to think, *How can he not remember the darkest day of my life?* I was in total shock. That was the last thing I expected him to say. So, I continued to describe to him in detail things he had done that he had forgotten and how his conduct that day was akin to what most people would consider torture.

By the end of our meal, I saw that my adoptive dad was mortified and had remorse for his actions.

I don't know if he truly had forgotten or repressed the details of what he did, or if denying a recollection was just choosing the coward's way out. Possibly he thought he was being recorded by me and didn't want an admission on record. Whichever path he was taking, it changed nothing about the past.

His intent in beating me was to get to the bottom of who did what to a toddler, but what he did was harm and scar his son based on an assumption.

At our breakfast meeting, I told him that for those eight years I lived under their roof I had believed he and his wife felt I was the worst child ever. Their regret for adopting me was obvious to me every day. I asked him, "Why did you make me feel that way all the time? What was I doing?" Even looking back, I still wondered what I had done that was so bad.

His answer to my question was to say, "Well, you lied to us all the time." But in his next breath, before I could even insert what I wanted to say, which was, "Well, why do you think that is?" he admitted, "But I know you did that because you were trying to survive me." He knew as well as I did that I would have to lie so he wouldn't beat me; and since everything I did was wrong in his eyes, I had to lie about everything.

After the breakfast with my adoptive dad, I felt better for one reason. I had always thought my adoptive dad was wiser than me. He got As and Bs in school. He was a respected businessman. He always used himself as a guide, "Look at me, be like me," while probably thinking I would never measure up to him. Thus, as a child, I had put him on a pedestal.

At the breakfast, he was still speaking to me like I was a child, yet I was thirty-eight at the time. He was trying to explain to me about forgiveness, when I stopped him and said, "I have no problem with forgiveness. I forgave all of my abusers a very long time ago. I asked you here to meet me because I have an issue I need you to help me resolve. I have a problem with what you did to me and I would like you to own up to it. I need you to listen, I need you to hear me. Whether you apologize or not, I need to be heard." That was the most important thing to me.

He still didn't get it.

From the meeting, I realized I was wiser than he was, wiser than a man I thought had set the standard on wisdom. That was a healing discovery for me. Going in, I wasn't entirely sure what I wanted to get out of the meeting. Mainly, I just wanted to become a stronger person for my son. What I did get out of the meeting in retrospect was the insight that I actually needed nothing from the man. I realized I could parent my son on my own just fine.

Everything I needed was already within me.

At the end of that meeting, we walked to our cars, hugged each other, and agreed to have breakfast once a year. We ended up only doing that one or two times more before I sued Arkansas for same-sex marriage rights. That's when he called me and asked me to change my last name. He didn't want to tarnish the Renegar name.

When I came out twelve years earlier, I was pretty sure his biggest fear was that I'd be running down Main Street in our small town wearing high heels and shouting our last name. I had been on the news in

Arkansas for two months and apparently his worst nightmare was unfolding.

He and my adoptive mom were religious Christians, and everyone where I grew up knew who I was and who they were. He was very upset by my lawsuit, and even offered to pay legal fees for me to change my last name. I declined the offer and after that we severed ties.

CHAPTER EIGHTEEN

Lights in a Dark World: My Heroes

It is important to surround yourself with people who like and love you because you're not going to like and love yourself every day. You'll need to rely on them from time to time.

I wouldn't have survived and thrived over the years without seeking out and surrounding myself with supportive people and tapping into the positive energy of those around me. Even throughout the worst times of intense darkness in my early years, some shining stars that helped change my stars found their way to me whom I will always think of as heroes.

The Crosswalk Lady

When we were foster kids, my sisters and I would walk down the hill from the Correlles' house to attend the

Lakewood Elementary School in Little Rock, Arkansas. I was about five at the time and there was a crosswalk with a crosswalk lady supervising it who was very nice to us. This lady was warmhearted and kind. She always met us with a smile and hugs. She'd let me hold the stop sign sometimes and I just thought that was absolutely everything! She also would stop and ask if we were okay and check us for wounds and bruises.

For my part, I wasn't sure why this crosswalk lady was always inspecting me so closely, looking down my shirt and pulling my winter jacket back to peer at my neck and shoulders. All I wanted to do was carry her stop sign. She was all love and totally sweet. The crosswalk was a very happy place for me. She really cared. Not only did she want to make sure we safely crossed the street but also that we were safe all the time, even at home.

Most days, she would walk with us and keep talking to us after we crossed. She even pulled my older sisters away and talked to them on their own to try to get more clarification as to why we always looked so battered and scared.

I remember thinking, *Oh God, I hope they don't say anything that gets us in trouble when we get home.* We had learned that lesson the hard way, many times. The Corelles had been reported for suspected child abuse eighteen times and apparently no one could save us from the unimaginable daily abuse.

I think the crosswalk lady may have reached out to another couple once she determined that our foster home was not safe. The husband in this couple was a pastor of a church and his wife was very pretty with long dark hair. A few times this couple would pull their car over and chat with us through their car window. It was obvious that they were fishing for clues they could use to tell the authorities.

One time we all got into their car. My sister had become familiar with them over the months and they drove us close to home but parked a couple of houses down. They turned in their seats to face us three in the backseat. They had given me a big Superman sticker and I was busy with that while they chatted with my older sisters. They asked us a bunch of questions about what was happening at the house. They were trying to pull answers from us, without alarming us.

Having been in similar situations in the past, my sisters and I knew what was happening and would never honestly answer questions like this because we would always get into bigger trouble at the house if our "tattling" was discovered. The odds of that happening seemed greater than the odds of us being saved, so we said as little as possible.

We were trying really hard not to tell these people anything, but I remember thinking they were sweet. They had won our trust. They figured it out and basically the message they were telling us was we were not alone. If we needed to tell someone, it was okay.

Shortly after this conversation, the cops came to the house again to do another investigation. Mrs. Corelle asked who we had spoken to and we didn't give any details. We moved houses soon after, but we never forgot how those wonderful people tried to help. Their message, "You are not alone," stayed with us.

Miss DeLeon, Our Concerned Neighbor

When we were living at the Corelles, my sisters and I would stop at our neighbor Miss DeLeon's house in the morning and walk her son to school with us. She was a young, tiny lady with a baby girl along with this young son. She always would ask us questions about what was happening. The police asked her questions after we were taken away as part of their investigation, but she wasn't someone we got close to—just a concerned neighbor.

Miss DeLeon placed many calls to social services to get us out of there, telling them she could hear our screams all the way from her house. Social services finally came to investigate and was assured by the Corelles that it wouldn't happen again. They were the only ones sure of it. Miss DeLeon was quoted to us as saying, "I don't understand why they would take those children away from their mama who beat them only to be put somewhere where they are beaten by all these other people." Her calls and testimony were part of the efforts that led to us finally being taken away and saved from that home. She remains in a special place in my heart for acting on her suspicions and being a responsible adult.

The English Teacher at the Children's Home

There was an English teacher who worked with the kids at the Children's Home the year that I started at Victorville Junior High School who wrote a story about me. She sent me a letter when I was twenty-two to let me know about a story she was writing about why she was going to give up teaching and retire because she was tired of her career, the kids were ungrateful, and no one wanted or seemed to learn anything. And then a cute, blond-haired boy walked in, came right up to her desk, and said, "Hi, I'm Cody Renegar." She ended up teaching for ten more years because I gave her hope.

She was a great lady. I remember handing her a picture of a rose I'd drawn when I introduced myself to her. We'd write a journal every morning and she would love to read my journal entries. I felt like she really connected with me. And she was safe. The fact that she had written a story about ME and how I changed her life meant so much to me. For the first time in many years, I felt wanted.

I connected with her recently by phone and we had a really nice chat. She said she thinks of me often and is extremely proud of who I have become. She said I had a huge impact on her life and that she was so glad that I walked in her classroom that day. It was really sweet.

Pete

At the Children's Home, when I was fifteen, where I lived after leaving the Renegars, a man named Pete was my house parent. There were five houses between which they split fifty-two kids and each home had a different parent. He stepped in like a father to me and made me feel genuinely loved. He was the first male in my life with whom I formed a healthy relationship and I really latched on to him. A man of kindness and goodness. He got divorced about three months after I moved in and became a single father to eight of us kids for two years. I stay in touch with him on social media.

When I decided to write this book, I asked Pete to share a story about his memory of me as a teenager and this is what he sent:

> I remember Cody coming to my cottage and being very young. I was glad to have him and, at first glance, I wondered why such a good-looking kid who seemed to be very sweet was coming to the Children's Home. Cody seemed very loving and caring and was always wanting attention. Especially mine. Cody was a very happy kid as long as he got a lot of my attention. I enjoyed spending

time with Cody, and in time, he became like a son to me.

I do remember that one time Cody went to Walmart with some other kids and got caught stealing a CD. He tried to put it down the front of his pants. I asked him why he tried to steal it, and he said, "To see if I could get away with it." Cody always had money, so money wasn't the issue.

I also remember that while Cody could be a very sweet and loving person, he could also push you to your limit. Which he seemed to do when he felt that he wasn't getting enough attention. I will never forget the time Cody pushed me to my max of anger. I always wondered what I would do if someone made me extremely mad. Well, Cody did it. We were standing in the hallway and Cody had gotten into trouble for some reason. I told him to go to his room and he kept fighting with me to the point where I lost it and started yelling as loudly as I could at him until I finished saying what I wanted him to hear and then I just stopped.

All of a sudden I was calm and thought, Well, that's all I got I guess. I looked at Cody and calmly said, "Go to your room because I don't want to talk to you anymore."

Cody looked at me and said, "That's not the way you are supposed to do it. You are supposed to take me to my room and sit down and talk to me."

I said, "I know, but that is what you want, to get my attention, so I'm not talking to you." You would have thought I beat him.

That was the only bad time that we had though. As Cody grew older and we spent more time together, he was happy and so was I. We became very close and, like I said earlier, he is like a son to me. He found his way into my heart and has been there ever since. So, when I talk about my kids, Cody is always counted as part of the family. I am very proud of the person that he has become. I love that he followed his dreams and worked so hard to accomplish his goals."

I'm so grateful that there are generous, caring people like Pete in the world.

The Horse Artist

I had neighbors with a lot of horses when I lived with the Renegars. David and Michelle Adams. They lived in a barn a few fields over from us and bought and sold horses for a living. Michelle, the wife, was an artist. She painted the most beautiful portraits of the many horses they owned. I considered myself an artist as well and she got me into painting horses, and I have never stopped painting ever since. For this reason, she will always hold a special place in my heart.

Michelle taught me how to turn my drawings into paintings and I thought she could do magic. She made a big difference in my life because art has been a passion and a comfort to me for thirty-seven years. Also, I am grateful to her because she tried to rescue me. She asked my adoptive dad if I could come live with her family because she knew he was abusing me. Once my adoptive dad knew that they were aware of the abuse he stopped me from going to their house.

Michelle had a room in her barn where she painted. I would sit there with her for hours and sketch my own stuff while she was painting, and the entire time we would have the best chats. I looked up to her so much because she was so kind—as was her husband, David. He was a real cowboy! No violence, no yelling, just calm, kind gentle people. They are still in Arkansas and still hold a special place in my memories. I am still in touch with them. And I still paint horses.

The Lane Twins

On my very first day in California, I met four people who remain my friends to this day. Two were the Lane Twins, Gary and Larry, who, as I mentioned earlier, ended up putting me in their documentary *Hollywood to Dollywood*. They had also previously won on the reality shows *Fear Factor* and *Wipe Out*.

When I met them, on the same night but at different times, I thought they were the same person. I was heading into a karaoke bar and Gary smiled at me outside on his cell phone. I walked inside and in a very short time Larry smiled at me from across the room and I thought, *How the hell did he get in here so fast?* Then Larry asked for my phone number and walked away. A short time later Gary asked and I'm like, "Didn't I give you my number already?" Then I realized they were twins.

The night I met the twins, I was with the only person I knew in L.A.. I had met Marco previously at a hair show and kept in contact with him. He told me he had an extra room that I could stay in when I got to California. When I arrived, I realized this was a lie. There was no extra room; he expected me to sleep in his bed. He thought he had just ordered himself a boyfriend, and I thought, *Crap! What did I get myself into?* So, we went out that night and I met the Lane twins and gave them my number—not in a romantic way, but just because we had a great connection. Marco, who was in a "jealous macho Latin" mood, saw me do this and got mad. His Latin accent was thick, especially when he would get mad. He was standing in the street outside the bar screaming at me, and I was like, *What is this guy talking about?* His accent got thicker and thicker the madder he got.

He said, "You need to get out of my house. I thought you were here to be my boyfriend."

I said, "I don't know what I did to make you think I'm here to be your boyfriend."

He took off and walked back to his house. The twins witnessed him screaming at me. I said, "What am I going to do?" I had saved enough for two months to be here, all I brought was a suitcase with some clothes and $2,000, that was it. They gave me a ride to where I was staying. As we pulled up, Marco was throwing all my stuff outside. The twins helped me pick it all up.

Gary and Larry came to my rescue that night and let me stay on their futon for two months while they were away, and then for another few months after that. Apparently that futon had many guests stay on it at various times over the years for extended stays. At least ten people besides myself. Their place was kind of like a hostel or an Airbnb before there were Airbnbs. The Lane futon was the place to stay when you were trying to make it in Hollywood and needed help.

I probably wouldn't have made it or had anything to do with L.A. after Marco kicked me out if those guys hadn't let me stay on the futon. I probably would have had to go back home. The arrangement worked out fantastically. Sometimes they would even have a job/gig and they weren't able to do it for some reason, so I would do the job in their place. Like doing a vodka promotion job at Hamburger Mary's or working as a bartender at a private party in Malibu. They threw me random little jobs because they knew I needed some money. I was living on savings after all.

Five years later I was in their movie when I was living back in Arkansas about an hour out of their way when they were driving to Dollywood in Tennessee.

They made a special stop to include me in the documentary. The Lane twins are good friends. I believe you must find good people and keep them in your life. We met for a reason. There's a reason our stars were aligned.

Melissa, Kim, Yvette, and Deepa

I posted this about my friend Melissa Langley on my Facebook page in 2019:

> *It feels like just yesterday (fourteen years ago) that I met this cutie at the country bar, and we have been side by side ever since! I didn't know how much I would need her strength throughout the years and have no idea where I would be if I didn't have this feisty li'l lady in my corner!! Thank you for all you've done in my life and for others my sweet, sweet friend!!! ALL MY LOVE, Mrs. Melissa. I am a better man because you came into my life.*

It's so important to have a circle of friends you can truly rely on especially during difficult times, part of a support group. Melissa is one of the most important people in that support group. Always there for me. Melissa and I did many protests together for causes like Marriage Equality, Don't Ask Don't Tell, and Prop 8. She is one of my biggest LGBTQ allies.

Melissa marched with me in many pride parades in Happy Valley, in fact the second year of their parade we led it. When Melissa and I are in a room full of people, sometimes everyone else just disappears. There could be one hundred other people in a bar but it's really just us. It's as if there is no one else in the place.

Melissa was one of the first friends I made when I made a conscious decision to cultivate friendships of substance, people that would be by my side no matter what I looked like or how much money I had.

I also met the lovely Kim Wright on the same night I met Melissa, and she also has remained a good friend to this day. We literally speak every day. She has a knack of bringing me out of my darkest moods and saddest moments with pure love. She is the self-appointed guardian of our circle; she is very protective of all her friends.

Yvette Wells, another friend from the same circle, forces me to feel attractive inside and out, even on days I'm not feeling that way. She can make me feel good-looking and like I'm a good person in a matter of moments. That's a rare talent which I appreciate.

Another true friend I met when I went to L.A., on my first day, was a truly amazing young woman who is still one of my closest friends. Deepa was an ambitious person who owned a hotel right in the middle of Hollywood. We connected instantly and decided that I would move into the room next to hers at the hotel. I got free housekeeping and breakfast and had no rent. And I was now living next door to my new best friend!

I asked Deepa to write a paragraph about her memories of meeting me and the time we spent together. This is what she wrote.

I met Cody one evening while I was catching a drink with a friend. He was very sweet and charming. The minute we met, I felt connected to him, as if we had known each other for years. After that day, we spent a lot of time together enjoying the city. We hiked, went out to karaoke, dined, and even attended a Deepak Chopra seminar in Carlsbad together for a week. I definitely feel Cody is one of my soul brothers, that we are always connected. When he moved back to Arkansas, it never felt like we lost touch. We are always able to pick right back up from where we last started. I've seen Cody go through his growth in L.A., from not knowing anyone to being surrounded by the "who's who" glitterati. The one thing I notice about him is his depth. He is a spiritually in tune man who functions out of love and the desire to connect. When around Cody, he will always make you feel like you're the most special, beautiful person in the world. I adore this quality about him. There isn't one incident I can think of when I've spent time with Cody and not laughed my face off.

David and Michael

I have never really had a father, but in the last ten years the universe saw fit to send David Russell into my life and he has been the most accepting, supportive, scolding when necessary, loving father I could ever have asked for! One gift that this crazy life has given me is that I am able to handpick my own family and he is the father I've always wanted.

I met my friend Michael Ron within just a few weeks of moving to Los Angeles when I was twenty-six years old! This man has an innate sense to know when my spirit is down, and he has always gone above and beyond to bring me back to life! He has flown me to Mexico many, many times, and to Vegas many, many times. He has taken me on cruises and on many friend dates! Everybody needs a party/travel buddy, and this man is that and so much more. He is my brother.

My Mentor, the Acclaimed José Éber

I want to tell you more about this man because he was such a positive influence on me. He gave me a chance, he gave me a lot of confidence, and he inspires me. He also taught me how to slow down and savor life a little. He took a liking to me and gave me the keys to the kingdom, so to speak, and I learned and learned from him and soaked up his expertise, doing all kinds of celebrity hair and having a blast. José called me the "Paris Hilton of the salon." He sent me to represent his salon on many red carpet events that he was invited to and couldn't attend personally. He passed down many invitations to me.

Tori Spelling told him I was the life of the party at one of the events, and after that, he gave me even more tickets to different events. José launched me into the world of being a celebrity stylist. He believed in me, which helped me believe in myself. Years after I left L.A. I saw him one day, and he said, "You just tell me when you're ready to come back."

I chuckle because he used to call me "Cody the Cowboy" because he thought I was so "country."

CHAPTER NINETEEN

Last Days with Mom

"There is always light, if only we are brave enough to see it. If only we are brave enough to be it."

—AMANDA GORMAN

Healing Someone Who Hurt Me

Mom never was able to process the rape from her father and uncle. It seemed like she was kind of in love with her dad to the end of her life, in a romantic way—to her, sex was love.

When my mom came and stayed with me when I was in my thirties, it was the first time she was truly open with me; her defenses were down, and she was actually willing to listen. I was older and wiser, and finally had the emotional tools and skills to speak to her. I think the universe brought her to me for those two months so that I could help her dissect all of the emotions and feelings she ever had and help her process her pain. At the end of our conversations, she said she understood the love of God. Before that, she just thought she was failing God. She owned a Bible and never really knew how to use it to pray or find peace.

I spent a lot of time showing Mom love through my eyes. I helped her heal and remember seeing such light in her. Every conversation we had, I would see a new light shining forth and for the first time in her life she was in a spiritual place and finally able to receive what I was saying. The words that were coming through me were not mine, however. It was more like our souls were talking and having an exchange.

If your soul has the information the person in front of you needs, it's going to come out. That's what happened on those nights on the porch while we were listening to the crickets and frogs and laughing together.

She told me that giving birth to me felt like giving birth to the sun. My delivery hurt her so much more than those of my two older sisters because I was a much bigger baby. She literally resented me for hurting her while she was giving birth to me and refused to hold me for three days because of that—once again displaying her undeniable lack of motherly skills.

She did love us, the only way she knew how. But she was too wounded and self-oriented to be a competent parent.

Mom's Death

After my mother left my home, I helped her get into an apartment about an hour away and was paying her bills and would go to visit her often. Then she started drinking again and I stopped going. I always made it a point that if she were drinking I would refuse to be around her. She was only four-foot-eleven, and she'd become kind of a little angry Yoda that I did not want to be around.

During this period of drinking, she got drunk and called me for several days in a row, leaving about fifty angry drunk messages. A roller coaster of voicemail. In some VMs, she was cursing and insulting me. In others, she was apologetic—in a childlike voice she would be begging me to call her back. I chose not to engage while she was on these drunken binges because nothing good ever came of it.

These calls came six months after she left my house.

A few weeks after receiving the calls I never answered, at the age of sixty-six, she was run over by a car while riding a bike at dusk. An elderly lady was driving who couldn't see her in the transitioning light.

My mom was lying in the street. The driver panicked and didn't even get out of the car. Instead, she called her son, an off-duty police officer who happened to be at a gas station around the corner. She didn't call 911. Even though it was an accident, this officer didn't want his mom to get in trouble for killing someone. He tried to sweep the whole thing under the rug. The local police department wouldn't give us a police report. Three weeks later, with our mom's body decaying in the morgue, we had to drive down to the police station, an hour from home, to tell them we needed a police report. That the coroner's office needed the police report to rule on the accident. It was almost two months after she died that we finally were able to have her cremated, which was her wish.

We went to the police station a second time. They never gave us anything. And so, we never really had a funeral because of this. We had no power.

Legally, police are supposed to provide their report within seventy-two hours. I hired a lawyer, but since Sue and I had been adopted by someone else Mom was no longer listed as our mother on our birth certificates.

Because my mother had very short hair at the time of her death, the initial news report put her down as a man. They posted a clip on the TV news showing her lying dead on the street. That broke my heart.

Not long after our mother's death, Sue was finally able to find some forgiveness for her, as shown in this poem she wrote and posted on her Facebook page.

Her Shoes Hurt

Never could I walk in the pain she carried in those shoes,

for it brought me to my knees.

Don't judge her without enduring her walk in life.

May the slippers she wears now be comforting.

Vivian Joyce Sandlin laugh like a child and love like an angel.

Now your pain is gone.

CHAPTER TWENTY

My Passions

"You know you're in love when you can't fall asleep because reality is finally better than your dreams."

—DR. SEUSS

Painting

One of my prides and joys, other than my husband, Terry, and my son and grandkids, is painting. I feel like creativity will well up inside of me and I have to get it out. I have started seeing everything as a painting and I've done hundreds of paintings.

The first time I ever drew something, I had seen a book with a picture of a boy riding a horse jumping over a log. I don't even know if I had ever seen a horse before this point but something inside me wanted to replicate this image so I could have it for myself. The foster home I was in at the time, the Corelles' house, was not at all conducive of children's creativity, so we did not have any art supplies. I looked in some books for a piece of paper that I might draw on and realized that in the back of every book is a protective blank piece of paper that I could tear out and draw on. So, I started drawing the picture inspired by the cover of that book with the boy riding the horse, and as I did, people kept coming by and giving me praise, saying things like, "Bravo," "Good job," and "You're really good." I thought *I'm gonna keep going if people are going to praise me.* One guy even affectionately ruffled my hair, so I kept drawing and drawing.

Something clicked in me that day and sparked my creativity. I can't think of a time that I had received praise before this. I'm sure there were moments, but none stands out. The attention and compliments that I was receiving meant I was loved, and it felt good getting praised rather than be hit for a change. With painting, I found my safe place within myself.

Ironic, isn't it, that the first thing I drew was a horse and continued drawing horses my whole life given that forty-two years later my long-lost cousin told me that I was named after her father's favorite horse, Cody?

I am in my forties now, and still have never taken official art classes of any kind, but art is my hobby. I draw a lot and paint lots of paintings and it is still my safe place. Painting is one of the main things that has helped me keep my sanity throughout this crazy life.

My favorite collection of my own paintings is a series I did of horses wearing wedding dresses. I heard someone say something about a famous actress having a "horse face" or a "face like a horse," using this comparison as a derogatory term. I hated the unkind intent behind the remark because my main passion is all about pride and making people feel amazing. I also hate that expression since horses are so beautiful.

Wanting to demonstrate how beautiful horses are, I painted a collection called "Relative Beauty" to show that beauty is in the eye of the beholder. In it, I painted many women with literal horse faces wearing beautiful clothing. To me, the women were beautiful.

Most of my work now is commissioned and in the last few years I have had a lot of requests for paintings of dogs because a magazine hired me to do a painting of Lisa Vanderpump's crazily Instagram-famous dog. After that, everybody, including many of her followers, started having me paint their dogs, which is fun. I can do dog portraits with my eyes closed though it's not my passion.

I've done some portraits of humans too, though I'm not a big fan of this because people don't usually see themselves the way others do or even how they are. They want you to paint them the way they look in their minds. Portraits are also a tricky thing for me because if I do them wrong, I'm afraid I'm going to make my subject feel ugly. I want to make them as beautiful or handsome as possible, but it has to look like them.

As I said, many people don't know how they look.

One of my biggest dreams is finally coming to fruition as I am making a name for myself as an artist and the value of my art is going up. I had never pursued painting as a career because I always heard the term "starving artist" when I was a kid. I thought to myself, *I want to be as far away from that as possible.* I wanted to be an artist but whenever I heard that term it took the wind out of my sails. It's what I wanted to go to school for, and my art was the only thing my adoptive dad was ever proud of me for—he thought it was cool to aspire to be an artist. He's a sculptor now himself in his retirement from the timber mill. He was trying to find the artist in himself at the time I lived in his home, so he was proud and enamored by my natural talent. I knew it was one of the rare times I would get praise from him for anything.

My artwork was picked up by an interior design company to have in their store, which also helped bring me some A-List celebrities as clients. My work has been featured on a couple of TV shows, too, including a reunion show of the original cast for *Queer Eye for the Straight Guy,* which aired in spring 2021.

Travelin' Man

In a relationship, you spend a lot of time trying to integrate your personality and wants with your partner's, trying to find common ground. When my relationship with Tony ended, I realized I had spent most of my life surrendering to someone else instead of figuring out who I was 100 percent.

I became very minimalistic after that discovery. I got rid of everything I had, taking my possessions all the way down to the basics. I didn't want clutter or extra stuff around me.

I used to go to the markets and fill my house with stuff like clothes. Today, I wear the same thing all the time. I don't have many clothes. I just do laundry frequently.

I've always wanted to see the world, and since my son is grown now, my minimalistic lifestyle allows me to do that more. It was easier to travel since I was living by myself and had completely downsized. I've always been open to people of different cultures, so my friends were surprised when I told them I hadn't been to Europe yet—hadn't even traveled across the sea. As soon as my son turned eighteen, I started taking trips.

There still is so much of the world I long to see and I want to see it all and understand humanity in all its aspects, which I hope can help me fully understand myself.

In the summer of 2019, I went bungee jumping off the side of a mountain in New Zealand. A few months later, I took an even bigger leap when I said yes to Terry's marriage proposal while dog sledding in Norway under the Northern Lights.

So far, my favorite country to visit was Spain. I have also been all over England and I'm crazy about it. My husband, Terry, is from there. On July fourth, he wishes me a happy "Ungrateful Colony Day."

One of my favorite places was New Zealand. One of my favorite things about it was the burgers. They make the most amazing, phenomenal hamburgers. We ate them every day while there. And I had been a vegetarian for about ten years before we went. Fergburger in Queensland was the name of the hamburger joint that finally knocked me off the veggie wagon. I should never move to New Zealand because I would eat those every day. I recall that I had lamb and venison as well as beef. Traveling made me a carnivore again.

I've now traveled to seventeen countries and thirty of the American states. Next, I'm planning to take a camel ride through Petra in Jordan, and drive from the south of France to Pompeii in southern Italy.

I use my traveling experiences as a goldmine. I have seen the world and met all kinds of people. There is a universe inside even the seemingly most boring person you come across; if you sit and really listen to them, there's so much to learn. Traveling is one of the most beautiful ways you can educate yourself and find your true skin.

With an open mind you can relate to, understand, and love other people from different cultures. You can't truly appreciate the culture in your town until you experience and compare it to other cultures.

Terry

Because I took time for myself, it helped me in my relationship with my Terry.

I'm more patient. Because I've figured out who I am, I'm comfortable with him being himself. We don't have to complete each other and all that stuff. I see him and if there's something that's bugging me about him that's one of his struggles, his challenges, I love him as he deals with it and goes through it, whereas before I would have thought, *We don't work well.* Now I also feel fine isolating myself if need be. I can let him have his own issues and processes because of my confidence in myself and my lovability. I don't have to fix him. I don't have to change him. He's on his own journey, his own path. He's pretty much perfect anyway if you ask me.

Terry is one of the most sought-after security consultants. I'm proud of myself for finally choosing someone extremely safe in comparison to my previous choices, a protector who is stable and strong. He's also handsome and very fit.

In previous relationships, I was always teaching my partners about the world and teaching them about my experiences. I then had a very clear thought during my period of self-discovery about the person I wanted to end up with. I wanted him to teach me because I wanted to learn new things. I wanted to be the one being inspired by someone else. I wanted someone to show me something I didn't know for a change. And boy has he.

Here is one of my recent Facebook posts.

Terry, three years today, baby!!!! It's been an amazing ride and we've overcome so many obstacles together, created some unforgettable moments, and I am forever changed because you care for my life and help me be a better version of me!! I love you angel!!!! I'm looking forward to many more memories together!!!

CHAPTER TWENTY-ONE

The Secrets of My Survival

*"You will continue to suffer if you have an emotional
reaction to everything that is said to you. True power is
sitting back and observing things with logic. True power is
restraint. If words control you, that means everyone else
can control you. Breathe and allow things to pass."*

—ANONYMOUS

How I Got Through It All

Imagination is a strong survival tool. My imagination
has always been the strongest and safest escape from
the harshness of my life since childhood and people
like the Corelles and my adoptive father. I was always
in the woods pretending I was someone else or
somewhere else. The animals and birds all had
personalities, they had life.

To this day, I love escaping in nature. It's always been a very soothing, healing thing for me to walk in the woods. Even just being barefoot in the grass helps me find peace. Letting a creek pour over my body washes all my problems away.

The property at my adoptive parents' house had a river near it. We had good times there as a family catching bass and mussels and grilling them over an open fire while camping on the tiny island in the river.

I've always allowed the power of nature to empower me.

My mother had the same capacity of escaping in her mind. Whenever I saw my mother go into her pretend happy place and become like a little girl, a girl who never truly existed, she was doing the same thing I have done with my art and my imagination.

My biggest secret for survival as a child was painting a picture of a world that didn't exist—a perfect picture of an imaginary safe place in my mind. I hid in my art—for instance, in a tree in a magic forest—until I could gain the strength to heal and deal with the reality of my situation and embrace the world I was living in.

Surviving the wilderness with my mother, bouncing from place to place with my siblings and her, like a small troupe of gypsies in southern Arkansas was an adventure. As miserable as it may seem in retrospect, to us kids that was just a normal way of life. We didn't have a lot to compare it to and we made the best of it. The things that people value that construct their comparison which tells them, "Gosh, that's awful," well, those are things they learned to value by being steeped in and nurtured by them, no differently than me.

Think about what your chores were when you were a child. Probably doing the dishes or making sure your dog had water or got walked, going to check the mail, or making sure there were no rocks in the yard before your father mowed it. I had chores too when I lived with my mom. I watched my little brothers. I got to roll up the knapsacks when we were on the move and find the boxes and bags we used to carry our things. I understood my responsibilities.

The pain in my stomach from being hungry didn't hurt nearly as much as watching my sisters groan in pain from their own hunger. My sisters would bring back pizza boxes and hamburger wrappers that I later learned were sometimes procured from a dumpster. Perhaps some of the food from the trash was even worse for our stomachs than hunger pangs.

We were being hurt often and I needed to protect my sisters and brothers, so we had a bond to survive and we were a team. These were my main thoughts. I knew that the people who were hurting us were hurt people themselves. I instinctively knew this, even at the young age of five and six. These people were damaged, and I was not damaged. (I was a baby.)

The main thoughts that got me through were that these people were damaged, *How can I help them? How can I protect my sisters and brothers?* and *How can this not harm me?* I was in survival mode, but my survival wasn't as much about surviving my physical and sexual abuse as it was about not wanting to come out of the scenario I was in and end up like the damaged people who were hurting me. I had an immense amount of love for some of these people, as well as sadness and compassion.

One time specifically that I recall from when I was a tiny child was when a big man with bright red hair was on top of me, rubbing his body against mine. I remember meeting his eyes and as soon as our eyes met, I thought, *This man is broken.* It seemed like everyone around me was broken, and I knew that the only thing for me to do was just hang on to the goodness I could feel inside myself.

I don't know why I had compassion for those who obviously didn't have any for me. I can't take credit for this. It was ingrained in me naturally and was perhaps my strongest tool for keeping rage and bitterness from growing in my heart.

Finding compassion for the people that hurt you is hard, but I never said this would be easy.

This works for me and allows me to be happy. I understood that what they were doing had nothing to do with me and wasn't about me, even though the behavior was directed at me. It was indeed hurting me to be used by sexual predators in these ways, but I was already a very strong child at this point. Tough. That's all I knew how to be.

Pain as a Comfort Zone

A month after I entered the Children's Home, my grades were all the way back up. I had As, Bs, and Cs and I was really happy. Even though the Home was a very strict religious environment, I wasn't being hit or degraded by my caretakers, so I started to thrive. (Roger's sexual advances came a couple years later, in my adolescence.) Initially, I was happy.

Too happy.

Let me explain what I mean by that.

I was raking leaves one day and found a piece of glass on the ground. I picked it up and started slowly pressing it into my wrist. I don't even know where the thought to do this came from or how it grew so quickly in my mind. I had never heard of "cutting." It was just a couple of spots of blood that I drew at first—and then I did the other wrist. I was mortified that I was doing this, extremely confused, and embarrassed to the point that I put on a long-sleeved shirt. The next day I did it again. For a while I wore long sleeves all the time.

I did this for a few weeks until my house parents saw the cuts and sent me to speak with the school's mental health counselor. The counselor's assessment was that for the first time in my life at the age of fifteen, I was not being hurt. I was happy and healthy. My grades had skyrocketed. I was becoming popular in school. I had lots of friends. Life was good. And my psyche didn't know how to handle not being in pain, so it was trying to get me back in my comfort zone of what was familiar—and all I had ever known was pain.

So, I hurt myself. I dug that piece of glass into my skin. The more it hurt, the better I felt.

Once the counselor told me why I was doing it, I stopped doing it. The explanation made sense. I learned that day that if I can get to the root of my pain and find out why it is happening and deal with it, it goes away. Or at least it gets filed away somewhere deep.

My house parents grounded me until I healed. Every day they would tend to my wounds, medicating and bandaging them with tenderness and patience, in turn showing me that I was safe without pain.

They helped me understand that I could live a life without pain. I still have scars from those weeks of cutting to remind me that I was able to overcome this challenge as well as the others.

The Secret of Reading: Books and Movies That Helped Me Heal and Understand

Reading books written by people who went through a similar upbringing as mine have helped me heal and rise above my circumstances. I will share a few of my favorites.

The Glass Castle. I loved and was inspired by Jeanette Walls' book *The Glass Castle*, which describes her childhood in rural Appalachia in extreme poverty. Even though the author as a child experienced many things a child shouldn't be exposed to, her childhood wasn't bad in her mind. She took the really crappy moments and put a positive spin on them the same way I always tried to do in the early years of my childhood. So, I could relate.

Walls' story had striking similarities to mine. As children, she and her multiple siblings were moved around a lot by their parents. They were extremely poor and often went without enough to eat. Many times, she and her brothers and sisters had to fend for themselves and take care of each other, because, like me, they had irresponsible parents.

Despite her upbringing, the author came out well-adjusted and became a successful journalist and author. A lot of people would think what that family and mine went through was a horrible thing, but we both looked at it as an adventure and chose not to be victims.

A Child Called It. Another favorite book of mine! As a boy, Dave Pelzer was abused badly. His was one of the worst cases in California history. He was placed in several foster homes and joined the army at eighteen. Again, someone I could relate to. The book showed me there are people out there who have had it way worse than me, and sadly, I suspect there always will be. The book really helped me put things into perspective. Before I read that book, I just thought I was dealt a tough hand. It also helped me realize that all the events in my life are in my past, far behind me. If anything is still lingering, it's my responsibility now to address it. I simply haven't found the strength to figure it out yet.

That book led me to realize I am in control of how I see my story.

If you choose to look at a situation a little differently, then the situation tends to change, and you can deal with it more easily. Perception is relative and you can find strength in habitual optimism. The key is repetition.

Pete's Dragon. This movie helped me to believe I was going to have a happy ending someday. It's about an eight- or nine-year-old kid who escapes a foster home that's a lot like the Corelles'. A dragon comes out of nowhere and helps him escape and becomes his advocate in life, helping him find a wonderful family before going on to help the next kid.

This story made me feel like there was someone out there looking for me who would help me and could lend me their strength to overcome my pain.

The Secret of My Religious Beliefs and Non-Beliefs

When I was fifteen or sixteen and living in the Children's Home, I often would study the Bible in my bedroom while my friends were outside playing. At one point, I began believing the strict religious ideas that were being fed to me by the staff at the school and thinking, *Maybe there's some truth to this.*

One day, I leaned back in my chair and closed my eyes and prayed, "Please don't ever let me lose the strength in my faith that I feel at this very moment."

The moment I sat forward, I opened my eyes with the sudden realization: *There's someone else on the other side of the world believing who knows what because that's the only thing they've ever been told or taught.* I saw that I almost fell into the same trap of believing without personal knowledge.

I decided to find out more for myself. I rode my bike daily to the library and was there for many hours reading several books on different religions, starting with Catholicism. One book would lead to another and I would study, study, study, feeling so fascinated. It quickly became a hobby to study theology. This hobby later took me to the Vatican in Rome, the Salt Lake (Mormon) Tabernacle in Utah and even to studying meditation under Deepak Chopra. I sensed there was something greater, a light in me that was going to explode if I didn't figure it out.

I was shown the exact nature of that light one night when I had a very beautiful personal spiritual experience with God. After that, I felt like that light inside me expanded. I now know that this light is truth, and it surrounds me. And protects me.

I found common ground in all those religions.

I also found my true belief. I believe what my God told me.

The Secret of My Sixth Sense

Sometimes survival mechanisms have downsides as well as upsides. When I get upset sometimes, I still don't always have the best tools to work with when I'm hurt. Instead, I do things like lashing out if I feel like I'm not being heard. I've gotten a million times better over the years, but I don't want to be that way anymore. I can really hurt someone with my words if I want to. I never want to.

Because I was surrounded by so many predators and abusers as a child, I had to quickly develop a sixth sense as to who was safe and who was not. This led me to being able to read people's weaknesses well. Because I was such a small child who couldn't fight back physically all I could use was my words. So, whenever I was angry, I knew how to cut people quickly to the bone. I realized when I got older and lost my temper several times that I had said things that I couldn't take back and the damage had been done. Now, no matter how mad I am at someone I don't want to hurt them. I've been able to mostly let go of that habit of wounding with words because I don't need it anymore.

Over the years, I've struggled a little with abandonment issues. When Terry and I had an argument or he got mad at me and went for a walk to cool down, it used to trigger me. Initially, I would worry that he was leaving me.

I had to figure out, *Why does this bother me so much?* My emotions were so heightened, and I didn't know why. A friend who knows me better than I know myself helped me realize it was due to my past.

Now, when Terry goes for a walk, I know he's coming back.

Let's Not Do Dinner

Because of the lack of true family structure in my childhood, I'm generally not comfortable sitting down at other people's family dinners. My friends used to always invite me over to their houses for Thanksgiving and Christmas, because they knew I didn't have family. I went a couple of times but found that I would get such anxiety that I have since refused.

I do not fault any of them! Although they were being kind to include me, I was simply seeing what I didn't have, and sometimes you don't know what you're missing until it's staring you right in the face. Sitting at the table, I would get what I can only describe as panic attacks. It was just such an unfamiliar situation.

Also, I guess I felt a bit like a pet orphan or a charity case. I didn't want pity from anyone.

When inevitably I would be asked questions about my own family, even though people's intentions were good, the simplest question led to a long, complicated, and awkward answer about my entire life story.

These days, when I go to dinners with the family of my husband, Terry, I feel like that's my family and that feels nice. I can also sit down with my sister Sue and her family, and I love that. What has helped me start being able to go to these places is that I have seen that there are no perfect families or houses.

Some families act phony when guests are around and try to pretend to be perfect. But I have realized these social facades are not true. I don't ever want to be fake in any way and I hope everyone feels comfortable being genuine with me too.

The Secret of Studying: Back to School

In 2019, I was hired for an ongoing job on the daytime TV show *The Talk*, a gig that required a cosmetology license, so back to school I went. This was a fun experience which led me to have a renewed faith in my skills. I absolutely didn't want to go back to school after doing hair for almost twenty-five years, but it was necessary for this amazing job opportunity. Before that, my license was as a barber.

I tried to pick the school with the least frills and up-charging for extras like supplies. I just needed the basic stuff to get through the state board test. I had three months in which to learn so much that I had never studied before. The things I learned there had to do with skin disease, nails, facials, and all of the nerves in the type of tissue surrounding each organ. The information was so anatomically detailed that I felt like I was in nursing school. I felt like three months would not be long enough.

I put all that I am into reading my textbooks and memorizing all sorts of crazy medical terms and had to perform services that I had actively avoided throughout my entire career. I ended up learning all that I needed to because of special attention I received from the four instructors at that school.

It was nice to know that I could, indeed, still learn new things and not just be stuck in a certain way of doing things. I also made some wonderful new friends in those three months, even though I originally went into the program with the mindset of not speaking to anyone and just getting through it. I love that I have a second license now, which gives me incredible confidence in what I do.

Funny. I didn't feel like that state board test was a test on the knowledge I learned in school, I felt like I was literally being tested by the universe to prove that I am who I have always said I am.

And I passed!

The Secret of Love: I Got Married!

Terry and I got married on July 18, 2020. I originally wanted to have a big celebratory wedding ceremony either on the beach or the cliffs in Malibu overlooking the ocean, and then to have another ceremony later on a farm in England. Then covid happened. We were originally planning an elaborate ceremony in the summer of 2021 but decided to move the date up as we were going to isolating together during the pandemic.

We found a small, tacky wedding chapel in a nearby town, where the only thing missing was an Elvis impersonator. The officiant kept saying, "We can't get started till the bride gets here." So, I jokingly said, "I am the bride."

She didn't understand right away, but then her granddaughter came over to explain it to her. Then she said, "Okay, we may begin."

We were there less than thirty minutes and it was done. Short and sweet.

We got off a plane from Florida, took rapid covid tests, went straight to the chapel, got married, and then were right back on a plane to Maine for the honeymoon. We were supposed to go to the South of France for our honeymoon, sail out to the Isle of Capri, then drive up the coast of Italy. We had to cancel that huge trip and instead we did a "six states in eight days" honeymoon tour of the United States that included a trip to Niagara Falls.

As always throughout my life, I rolled with it. I never have any high expectations that I can't get out of. Sometimes the stars get crisscrossed temporarily. Things change, I change, our honeymoon plans changed, but I still got to marry the sweetest man I've ever known.

When it's safe and covid is conquered, we are still planning a ceremony in the United Kingdom on the 700-year-old farm turned into a bed and breakfast that has become our special place. We've stayed there three times. Our close friends and family, including Sue and her kids, will join us from all over the world.

CHAPTER TWENTY-TWO

The Way to Change Your Stars

"Just because it's written in the stars doesn't mean you can't erase it."

—SUDI "RICK" KARATAS

Tell Your Story

Through telling my story and others telling theirs, we can be part of a chain of healing. Since I had such a violent childhood and then went straight into being a father, I feel like I never truly had a childhood, and this has given me a very different outlook on the world as an adult in my forties. I see the world through a child's eyes as well as with the wisdom of my experience, so therein lies another beautiful gift I've received.

Feelings can be gifts. Feeling every emotion, being aware of them, and being present for them is important. This includes crying, being angry, and being sad and horribly distraught, as well as laughing, loving deeply, and loving the tiniest and largest of all things. The capacity to love is a gift each of us has inside us.

My eyes and heart are completely wide open at any given moment. To be that raw and vulnerable gives me strength. You can't experience lightness without darkness, right? The yin without the yang. The ebb without the flow. All of it. None can exist without its opposite.

I feel so deeply the beauty of it all because I felt so deeply the pain of it all, from the shattered glass I once was forced to walk through. The pain was the foundation for the rest of my beautiful life. It's all a glorious and grand gift from the powers beyond my soul and I'll be forever grateful for every moment and every breath.

I think that traveling the world and stepping out of this incredibly young country that the universe saw fit to have me born in has given me perspective that I would not have had otherwise. Seeing the old streets and buildings in other countries and seeing the absolutely ancient lives of those who came before us long ago reminds me how fleeting a life is and (not to be cliché) how insignificant we all are, if we choose to be. Insignificance is a choice! As is significance.

If you feel too small, too powerless, or unhappy, then make a change however you can. At the very least, tell your story. There is someone out there living a similar life and grasping, and desperately reaching out a hand, for someone, anyone, to tell them they are okay and do belong here. Maybe by sharing a little bit of our own lives, we can plant tiny seeds of hope and inspiration and knowledge in the lives of others.

We are all, absolutely, in this game together. Why shouldn't we choose to help each other? I can't think of a reason. And honestly, if you can think of a reason not to help someone, then you are probably not healed. But hopefully, by this point, you are beginning to see things from a different perspective and are on your way.

Why would I ever think that just because I was younger than my attackers I wouldn't be wiser than them? Who says age makes us wiser? I've always wondered why I understood, at such a young age, what was happening and had pity on those that hurt me. It's not true that older people always understand things better than younger people.

My soul collects the gifts of personal experience like pearls of wisdom. I use these experiences for personal growth and gift them to others who may one day need to call on them. My weaknesses have become my strengths.

Life can be glorious if you don't hold back! Celebrate yourself and all your magnificent flaws!

Be Like Buddha

In my twenties, I was getting into a lot of bar fights and blew up at a lot of different things that didn't call for that type of reaction. These anger issues followed me into my thirties.

Subsequently, I chose to let go of my anger because it was only poisoning me. No reason for me to hang on to anger that was only doing damage to me rather than those I came in contact with. As the Buddha said, "Holding onto anger is like drinking poison and expecting the other person to die."

But first I had to investigate where this unwelcomed emotion—this anger—was coming from. I made a conscious choice to release those emotions and focus only on moving forward without the extra baggage. Then, I went through a list of all my abusers in my head, recalled how their violations made me feel, and asked my soul why that anger was still there.

I'm not a naturally angry person.

I wondered, *What would I do if I ever saw those guys?*

I got my answer recently when I found out that one of my abusers was homeless in Denver, Colorado. To my surprise, my first thought was. *I need to go find him and help him. I need to make sure he has shelter and food.* All the personal growth work I'd focused on for so long had truly paid off. The fact that my reflex was to help him, instead of plan my revenge on him, was a huge clue to me that I am indeed healed.

Bringing Joy to Others

For the show *The Talk*, I worked as Marie Osmond's hairstylist briefly. What I discovered in the process is that I really love to bring joy to others. I have a real gift for that. I've always been told yet I never fully understood it until that show. I brought joy to almost everyone involved. People would stop me and say, "Wow, you've changed the show."

Marie said, "You brought fun to this. You brought joy back into my job. I've prayed for thirty years that you would come into my life." I was in my forties by this point and her statement made me realize I had been attempting to bring joy to others my whole life.

I would get to work an hour early and prepare by trying to get my energy up before Marie walked in the room so I could share that energy with her and everyone on the set. I saw so many deeply dark, sad souls there. The universe has given me a gift to share light and joy. I made a point to always be 100 percent present and take advantage of every moment working on that show to be a beacon of light.

Marie Osmond has become a good friend. She asked me to do her portrait and teach her to paint.

Keep Moving, Be a Shooting Star

I've never been stagnant. I never thought, *This is it* or *This is all there is.* I believe many people think that where they are is as far as they can go. I want people to believe they are never as far as they can go. Nothing wrong with being content where you are as long as it's a healthy place. But you can always dream a little bit more if that's what you desire. Those that want can go further. Be and do a little bit more and always better yourself.

I've been active my whole life in the quest to find the things that hurt me and heal from them. Otherwise, I would just be carrying painful muck for the rest of my life. Muck that's heavy. It's hard to be happy when carrying extra weight. I actively try to identify my faults so I can get rid of them. I'm still working on myself and hopefully always will be. Self-improvement is a hobby I enjoy.

My childhood gave me an interest in traveling and a sense of adventure that I have brought into my adult life. So, this was a benefit. Being in different homes and traveling, adventure always found me. Also having a mother with a nomadic spirit was a gift.

That's how I choose to look at it.

As an adult, I have come to believe that traveling is one of the most important things we can do. It's educational. Also it's one of the best things we can do for the soul; meeting different people and learning about different cultures is soul expanding. It opens our minds and hearts and teaches us to be tolerant and respectful.

Tiny Choices Make a Big Difference

Whether it was a good one or bad one, most of us spend the rest of our lives emotionally revisiting our childhood. How we're raised and the experiences we have shape us in many ways because our brains are malleable and as absorbent as sponges when we are young. How we let it shape us beyond childhood is up to us. In my experience, there's so much that is controlled by our choices, and our choices alone. For example, we don't have to relive our memories and the pain we've felt every day in any way that we don't want to. We can intervene to reframe our thoughts, focus on something else, or slow our thoughts down so we can integrate the pain and give it meaning.

If you've had a painful past like mine, you can choose to stand tall and breathe through the dark times and to be strong for yourself and for others in the good times. Every tiny choice you make adds up quickly. You absolutely have to be aware of what you're choosing and to make your choices intentional. If you are reliving those moments and choosing to have the exact same emotional response that you had at the beginning, then that's what you're going to get. And there's no light at the end of that particular tunnel.

I suggest that you make it a habit to choose happiness, healing, and forgiveness with every breath you take.

These choices rarely present themselves as big, monumental decisions. Most of the time, it is in the tiniest of moments that you have to make the most significant decisions. If you pay close attention and you are able to be aware of the intention to choose happiness, and hold onto this thought every day, then, like anything else, it will become a habit. You will slowly feel that darkness above your head becoming sunshine and the weight on your shoulders becoming lighter.

Beautiful things will happen to you if you choose healing with every single choice you make. Otherwise, you are subconsciously, or even consciously, choosing to stay a victim. You are choosing that.

You have many, many small choices to make. Choose wisely.

What Might Have Been

I found out recently from a cousin that a few years after my mom had left my dad, when we kids were taken away from her and put in foster care, the DHS had found my father and called him. My cousin answered the phone. They told my cousin to tell my dad that they found his kids and how we had been in and out of some horrible situations and were looking for him. Apparently, she put her hand over the receiver and told my dad just that.

He responded by saying, "Leave it."

She asked, "What do you mean, 'Leave it'?!"

He then stood up from the table, walked over, took the phone out of her hand, and placed the receiver back on the wall mount.

He had the chance to take us in and didn't at that time.

Our whole lives could have been completely altered had he taken that call. But whether for better or worse, who knows?

ABOUT THE AUTHOR

Cody Renegar is a hairstylist and fine artist. He currently lives in California with his husband, Terry. He has a son, Levi, who, with his partner, Alaya, has given Cody three grandkids. Cody is the hairstylist of choice for many Hollywood entertainment industry celebrities and A-listers. Los Angeles is his main stage although he also maintains a large clientele in Washington, D.C., and Arkansas. He is a cosmetologist and master barber with twenty-five years of experience with unique cutting styles and techniques, and a former cutting director for Aveda and Bumble & Bumble, Minneapolis. Cody began his career in 1996 in Arkansas. He moved to José Éber Salon on Rodeo Drive in Beverly Hills in 2004, where he had the honor of working alongside José on the main floor and in his private styling room, working with many high-profile clients. Cody has been featured in the documentary film *Hollywood to Dollywood* and the book *Rainbow Relatives*. A talented artist, Cody's paintings hang in private collections around the world.

Made in the USA
Las Vegas, NV
12 March 2021